HELL NO

Also by Michael Ratner

Killing Che: How the CIA Got Away with Murder
(co-author with Michael Smith)

The Trial of Donald Rumsfeld: A Prosecution by Book

Guantánamo: What the World Should Know
(co-author with Ellen Ray)

The Pinochet Papers:
The Case of Augusto Pinochet in Spain and Britain
(co-editor with Reed Brody)

International Human Rights Litigation in U.S. Courts
(co-author with Beth Stephens)

HELL NO

Your Right to Dissent in Twenty-First-Century America

Michael Ratner and Margaret Ratner Kunstler

in conjunction with the
Center for Constitutional Rights

THE NEW PRESS

NEW YORK
LONDON

"The Meaning and Importance of Dissent" © 2011 by Michael Ratner and
Margaret Ratner Kunstler

"If an Agent Knocks" was originally published in 1984 (3rd edition, 2009)
by the Center for Constitutional Rights and is reprinted here with permission.

Requests for permission to reproduce selections from this book should be
mailed to: Permissions Department, The New Press, 38 Greene Street,
New York, NY 10013.

Published in the United States by The New Press, New York, 2011
Distributed by Perseus Distribution

LIBRARY OF CONGRESS CATALOGING-IN-PUBLICATION DATA

Ratner, Michael, 1943–
    Hell no : your right to dissent in 21st-century America / Michael Ratner,
Margaret Ratner Kunstler.
        p.   cm.
    Includes bibliographical references.
    ISBN 978-1-59558-540-0 (pbk.)
    1. Freedom of expression—United States—History.   2. Government,
Resistance to—United States—History.   3. Civil rights—United
States—History.   4. Dissenters—Legal status, laws, etc.—United States—
History.   5. United States. Federal Bureau of Investigation—History.
I. Ratner Kunstler, Margaret.   II. Title.
    KF4770.R38 2011
    342.7308'5—dc22   2011012996

The New Press was established in 1990 as a not-for-profit alternative to the large,
commercial publishing houses currently dominating the book publishing industry.
The New Press operates in the public interest rather than for private gain, and is
committed to publishing, in innovative ways, works of educational, cultural, and
community value that are often deemed insufficiently profitable.

www.thenewpress.com

Composition by dix!
This book was set in Minion

Printed in the United States of America

10   9   8   7   6   5   4   3   2   1

CONTENTS

PREFACE

Vincent Warren

"Terrorism" is a word that has been used repeatedly by the executive branch since 9/11 to provide a rationale for going to war; unlawfully wiretapping, indefinitely detaining, and torturing people; and cracking down on protest and dissent in violation of the U.S. Constitution and international law. The executive branch of the government—and I am sad to say this includes both the Bush and the Obama administrations when it comes to most of these issues—has ushered in a new era of repression, enabling law enforcement agencies to abuse their powers by targeting, detaining, and silencing political activists. History demonstrates that this type of repression is far from a new exercise for the government. However, the current national security state has a cherished and enduring ally: the collective, overpowering fear of violent terrorism and the desire for the government to keep us safe.

With the killing of Osama bin Laden in Pakistan, many are asking what the effect on our war-making foreign policy with respect to terrorism will be. That is only part of the question we should be asking. As this book makes clear, the other question is: what effect will our war-making foreign policy continue to have on our protest of that policy?

I believe the answer is that unless and until the United States stops its current policy of declaring war on anyone in the world in the name of combating terrorism, people will continue to organize themselves to oppose it. And as long as people oppose antiterrorism policies, the government will use its power to label dissenters as terrorists. Finally, as long as the people remain afraid of the supposed terrorists in our midst, the activists—those we rely on to protest illegal and unjust government activities—will find it exceedingly hard to spread information about what the government is doing in our name.

This book outlines the work that the Center for Constitutional Rights (CCR) and many others have done to identify and combat illegal surveillance and infiltration of activists, the crackdown on protests, and the criminalization of lawful political activity. It also offers the reader a range of tools to use when that political activity piques the interest of law enforcement. It chronicles the evolution of repressive laws and tactics aimed at disempowering those who invoke our basic rights to speak, assemble, and demand redress from the government.

It also speaks to the current state of dissent and notes that, while the stakes for defending dissent couldn't be higher today, the obstacles are more difficult and more complicated. Much of the organizing occurs online and by mobile phone and computer. This makes organizing more effective for the activists, but it also makes it easier for law enforcement to spy on and disrupt the activists' plans. For example, law enforcement has established "Joint Terrorism Task Forces" that bring together federal, state, and local law enforcement and other agencies into "fusion centers." State governments are even contracting out their illegal surveillance to private companies, as was done recently in Pennsylvania, when state homeland security director James Powers hired a private company to research and distribute information about groups engaged in lawful activity.

Moreover, activists today run the very real risk of being arrested and prosecuted for their First Amendment activity under so-called material support laws, a danger made more real by the 2010 Supreme Court ruling in a Center for Constitutional Rights case, *Holder v. Humanitarian Law Project (HLP)*. CCR challenged the material support statutes, including a portion of the USA PATRIOT Act, which make it a crime to provide support—including humanitarian aid, literature distribution, and peaceful political advocacy—to any entity that the government has designated as a "terrorist" group. The Court ruled that human rights advocates providing training and assistance in the nonviolent resolution of disputes can be prosecuted as terrorists. While activists and the legal community are still trying to figure out the limits of the HLP case, it has brought a chill on protected activity. The Court has criminalized speech and given the government more power to prosecute peace activists and human rights organizations who engage with groups on the government's list even to support lawful goals.

A national security state is a difficult place to protest. Yet, without that protest, the "War on Terror" framework that swings indiscriminately between terrorist suspects and peace and justice activists will be with us forever. No president in history ever weakened his powers, and it is not likely to happen in the future. To the contrary, we can count on the government to fiercely resist all of our efforts to change its policies, make it more transparent, and hold its officials accountable for the crimes they have committed. As a result, there is a more urgent need than ever for people of conscience to stand up and say "Hell No" to war-making, torture, indefinite detention, extrajudicial killing, and racial profiling, among many activities that the government currently does with impunity. We need to say loudly and clearly that political dissent is not criminal activity, protest is not terrorism, and that the current national security state must be dismantled.

May 2011

AUTHORS' NOTE

This book addresses new and increasing government limitations on the right to protest and to seek social and political change in the United States—to examine the state of dissent in the twenty-first century. The opening section offers a broad overview of the history of dissent—highlighting instances in which it has brought about change and also those in which such dissent has been effectively suppressed—while emphasizing the legal environment that has developed since 9/11. Today there is widespread targeting of activists by the FBI and other government agencies, and this section offers an attempt to document surveillance and disruption of protest, often carried out under the guise of investigating supposed domestic terrorism.

The next section explains some of what can be done in response. It offers hands-on advice for dissenters, activists, and protesters engaged in the issues facing the country today. It provides concrete suggestions for dealing with police and FBI actions ranging from street encounters to spying, infiltration, grand jury subpoenas, and the execution of search warrants. Special features focus on electronic communications, issues faced by noncitizens, and international travel. It is meant to serve as a guide to help organizations and activists be fully informed and

protected in the event of government interference with
protest, activism, and dissent. This section is provided for
informational purposes and does not constitute legal advice. Our aim is to provide a general description of the
legal and practical issues that progressive or radical activists may face, with the understanding that each person's
circumstances are unique, and minor factual differences
may result in different answers to the questions presented
in this segment of the book. It is important to remember
that different states have different laws—so it is a good
idea to learn the laws of your state and to have access to a
lawyer who is familiar with them. Finally, the book con-
cludes with a reprint of the 2008 Mukasey FBI guidelines,
which regulate the government's response to dissent in the
twenty-first century.

Our hope is that this book will prepare people to speak
out, take action, and, by doing so, turn the tide against the
increasing repression faced by those who dare to dissent.

I.

THE MEANING AND IMPORTANCE
OF DISSENT

Many of us think of the constitutionally protected right to dissent as the right to speak our minds and write and publish what we think. But free speech is only one of three related rights protected by the First Amendment. Not only is Congress prohibited from passing a law "abridging the freedom of speech, or of the press," the amendment also protects "the right of the people peaceably to assemble" and their right "to petition the Government for a redress of grievances."

Taken together, the right to free speech, the right of assembly, and the explicit right to express grievances to the government add up to an expansive right to "dissent" enshrined in the Bill of Rights. Beyond written or spoken words, the right to dissent is the right of citizens to organize themselves, to associate, to make themselves heard in order to achieve political and social change and oppose government policies without fear of impediment or reprisal.

Despite these clear protections, the government has not always lived up to its constitutionally required mandate to protect our right to dissent. Indeed, it is this right that the government, whether federal, state, or local, has typically targeted for repression, especially in times of claimed "emergencies." That has been true historically and it is true today. Often, federal agencies and state and city governments, at times of both war and relative quiescence, try through surveillance, infiltration, and limits on protest to suppress dissent. Most of these repressive efforts have ultimately been beaten back, but not before people were jailed, and often not until the effects of the claimed "emergency" that purportedly justified the restrictions had dissipated.

Since the founding of this nation, the government has made many efforts to restrict free speech and dissent. The list on page 8 is a cursory overview of major turning points in the history of attacks on dissent. The rest of this chapter provides a more in-depth look at the continued assault on our right to dissent over the past fifty years, with a special focus on the new post–9/11 legal framework.

It is important to note that government measures limiting organized dissent have become increasingly common in our society since the terrorist attacks of 2001. These assaults upon and criminalization of dissent— from the surveillance of activists to the federalization of local law enforcement to the labeling of activists as "terrorists"—dismantle piece by piece a core right considered essential to meaningful democracy. Understanding the evisceration of this right is a first step to regaining our lost liberties.

BRINGING ABOUT POLITICAL
AND SOCIAL CHANGE

Free speech is a bedrock principle of our nation. The Framers believed that open and unfettered discussion would promote better thinking and decisions, particularly important when it came to government policies. The Supreme Court stated in 1964 in *New York Times Co. v. Sullivan*, a seminal case on modern-day dissent:

> The general proposition that freedom of expression upon public questions is secured by the First Amendment has long been settled by our decisions. The constitutional safeguard, we have said, "was fashioned to assure unfettered interchange of ideas for the bringing about of political and social changes desired by the people."

This "unfettered interchange of ideas" on public issues, according to *Sullivan*, must be "uninhibited, robust, and wide-open . . . [and] it may well include vehement, caustic, and sometimes unpleasantly sharp attacks on government and public officials."

Clearly, the lone speaker standing on a soapbox in Times Square or the odd local newspaper article opposing a war will generally not lead to change in government policy. It has always been understood that the right to speak freely is not sufficient without the ability to make that speech effectively reach a meaningful audience. That is why other related rights are included in the First Amendment. Congress was prohibited from abridging the right to demonstrate ("people peaceably to assemble") and from interfering with the right to petition and lobby government officials ("petition the Government for a redress of grievances"). Implicit in the rights to assemble and petition is the right to freedom of association—the right to join together with others to advocate for change. The Supreme Court has recognized this right of association as a critical part of First Amendment protections.

While not literally protected by the First Amendment, civil disobedience and passive resistance fall within its broad ambit. They are often found to be effective expressions of political dissent because such tactics are a source of organizational solidarity and attract wider media attention. For people without the means to purchase airtime or newspaper space, organized protest offers a chance to "speak with their bodies" and collectively to make themselves heard.

Protesters typically break the law in insubstantial, generally nonviolent ways while making clear that their technically illegal actions seek to bring about change in policies or practices that are much more harmful than these actions. Such minor violations of law have a long and honorable history in this country. Thousands of activists engaged in civil disobedience in the South to break the Jim Crow laws. Hundreds today engage in civil disobedience protesting the Guantánamo Bay detention camp, torture, draconian immigration laws, and Appalachian mountaintop removal.

Sometimes, however, these minor violations are dealt with severely so as to discourage effective protest. We saw this in the South with mass arrests and jailings meted out to Dr. King and others. We are seeing it today with special laws that treat acts of civil disobedience as terrorism and single out environmentalists for especially harsh sentences. Such repression is never about the nature of the legal violations; it is always about discouraging vigorous dissent and protecting governmental and corporate interests.

Other amendments in our Constitution also ensure that these speech protections can be used effectively. The Fourth Amendment ensures that our persons, homes, and places of work are not searched without good reason (searching homes and offices for evidence of dissent is one way governments have historically tried to impede free speech) and that our various forms of communications are protected from unwarranted surveillance. The Fifth Amendment guarantees us due process of law before we can be imprisoned or held liable and is designed in part to stop government from using imprisonment as a means of suppressing potential dissent.

Even a cursory look at struggles for progressive social change in America reveals the wisdom of viewing the First Amendment in the context of protecting direct advocacy of social and political change. Often change has occurred only when free speech is taken to the streets, when thousands and eventually millions of people force their demands upon the government and compel the government to act and to change. That is how women gained the right to vote, labor won the 40-hour workweek and the right to unionize, the civil rights movement in the 1950s and 1960s overcame the segregation policies of Jim Crow, protesters helped bring an end to the Vietnam War, and millions in the United States and around the world tried to prevent the 2003 Iraq war. That is why today immigrants and their supporters are marching in demand of immigration reform.

There are some who believed that the access to information provided by the Internet would provide a new force for change—that the democratization of information sharing would provide a new means of association and organization by which to foster political and social change. While access to the Internet has allowed countless voices to speak, the very proliferation of voices means that few are heard by large numbers of people. Neither does the Internet alone provide the real social connectedness needed for political organization. A YouTube video or a blog post can certainly spark action, but as we saw throughout North Africa, change comes about when people take to the streets.

Protests, while often having an element of spontaneity, need organization to be effective. This organizing often begins with small activist groups who believe that protest against unjust policies and practices is a necessity, and that activism in support of just and moral policies is an obligation. The Student Nonviolent Coordinating Committee, the Southern Christian Leadership Conference, and other activist organizations led civil rights protests in the South; the National Mobilization Committee to End the War in Vietnam (a coalition of many groups) led protests against that war; ACT UP organized to draw attention to our government's failure to respond to the AIDS crisis; dozens of groups concerned by the draconian 2010 anti-immigration law in Arizona protested in almost 50 cities against that law. These groups formed and were able to function because the First Amendment forbids the government from interfering with their right of association. Too often, however, the history books omit that, at the time these protests occurred, they met strong, even violent resistance from the government and parts of the public.

DISABLING DEMOCRACY: THE ATTACK ON DISSENT IN AMERICA

The U.S. government has regularly sought to suppress movements for social change that challenge the status quo, the hierarchy of power, and the impunity of corporations. This suppression has waxed and waned based on various factors, including the strength and popularity of such movements. Despite the widespread heralding of First Amendment rights, U.S. history includes numerous examples of government authorities using surveillance, spying, wiretapping, infiltration, entrapment, criminal prosecutions, and even extrajudicial homicide to try to suppress dissent and its public expression. The targeting of movements, organizations, and individuals seeking social and political change has taken many forms, including denying demonstrators permits, restricting demonstration sites, controlling the media, and harassing participants, often involving tax audits and character assassination. Historically the government has used both legal means such as search warrants, grand jury subpoenas, indictments, and trials as well as illegal means such as infiltration and entrapment to hinder, if not destroy, its opponents.

- **The Sedition Act (1798)** (allowed to expire in 1801, but considered unconstitutional by later courts) made it a crime to criticize the government.
- **The Espionage Act (1917)** made it a crime to incite disloyalty or advocate against military recruitment. Courts have since cast doubt on the constitutionality of its speech provisions.
- **The anticommunist Palmer Raids (1919)** combined executive action with legislation to crack down on and deport radical leftists and immigrants, actions subsequently revoked by the secretary of labor.
- **The Special Committee on Un-American Activities (1934)**, which later became the House Un-American Activities Committee (HUAC), was a congressional committee devoted to investigating political thought that subsequently imprisoned people who refused to answer questions about their political affiliations.
- **The preventive internment of more than 120,000 Japanese citizens and residents during World War II** exemplified wartime excesses in racial profiling, preventive detention, and violation of civil liberties. It was later ruled by the Supreme Court to be unjustified.
- **COINTELPRO (1950s–1970s)**, the FBI's secret intelligence program, illegally targeted various individuals and groups including Dr. Martin Luther King Jr., the Southern Christian Leadership Conference, the Black Panther Party, the American Indian Movement, Daniel Ellsberg, and many others in the name of monitoring potential "threats."
- **The Antiterrorism and Effective Death Penalty Act (1996)** created a new category of prohibited activity: "material support" to groups designated by the State Department to be Foreign Terrorist Organizations (FTOs), including a range of groups sharing a common opposition to U.S. foreign policy. Enacted in the wake of the Oklahoma City bombing, this act contained little to no content relevant to the circumstances that produced it.

- **The USA PATRIOT Act (2001),** containing laws of questionable constitutionality, expands government surveillance powers, erodes the right to habeas corpus, formalizes the use of military tribunals rather than courts in the judicial branch, and allows the use of coerced testimony and torture as part of military prosecution techniques. Under this act, much of what has been traditionally considered standard civil disobedience is now viewed as terrorism.
- **The TALON databases (2003),** part of the increased federalization of local law enforcement, were purportedly set up by the Defense Department to monitor potential threats to the department's quarters within the United States. However, Freedom of Information Act (FOIA) requests, lawsuits, and media coverage have shown that the Defense Department went well beyond its stated mission, executing sweeping surveillance of a wide variety of peaceful political activities and meetings rather than adhering to the mandate to collect information on an alleged "threat" and judge it to be either "credible" or "not credible."
- **The Animal Enterprise Terrorism Act (2006)** amends the Animal Enterprise Protection Act by increasing the penalties for activities that disrupt the business of companies that exploit and abuse animals, and broadens the scope of businesses that the law protects. The law deters protests, leafleting, boycotts, and joining animal rights organizations by using broad language that induces fear of being labeled a "terrorist," and federalizes penalties for civil disobedience–type actions that were previously classified as minor crimes and prosecuted under state law.

A wide range of dissenting activist groups in the 1960s and 1970s were subject to infiltration, spying, and persecution. Some of the worst misdeeds of the FBI came out of a counterintelligence program dubbed COINTELPRO, which targeted black-led civil rights groups for destruction. As documents have become available over the years, it has become clear that COINTELPRO also targeted Puerto Rican *independentistas,* communists, the New Left, the American Indian Movement (AIM), the National Organization for Women (NOW), and others.

The program began in 1967, when FBI director J. Edgar Hoover, responding to what was perceived as the growing threat of the civil rights movement, expanded the FBI's already-existing covert program to "neutralize" African American organizations and their leaders. On August 25, 1967, Hoover instructed 22 FBI field offices to commence a counterintelligence program designed to "expose, disrupt . . . and otherwise neutralize Black organizations and their leadership." In 1968, COINTELPRO was expanded to 43 field offices nationwide. Significantly, while the FBI often claims that one of COINTELPRO's goals was to prevent violence, one of the program's initial targets was the Rev. Dr. Martin Luther King Jr., a winner of the Nobel Peace Prize and a worldwide advocate of nonviolent social change.

By late 1968, the Black Panther Party became the main target of COINTELPRO. Director Hoover ordered all field offices to submit regularly "hard-hitting counterintelligence measures aimed at crippling the BPP." The BPP's Ten Point Program argued for complete control of black communities by blacks, for an end to "robbery by the capitalists," an "end to all wars of aggression," and freedom for "all oppressed and Black people." Beyond their written words, it was the Panthers' organizing and public protests that drew attention and led to the group's being infiltrated, jailed, violently attacked, and ultimately destroyed by the government.

Heavy-handed government repression is not always successful. It has even been known to backfire. Sometimes the protesters prevail despite government repression. So, for example, the FBI's failed efforts to disrupt the Southern civil rights movement are well documented: the bureau infiltrated the civil rights organizations, had plans to kill black leaders, and participated in violent acts against protesters. The movement against the Vietnam War similarly prevailed, despite Richard Nixon's efforts to disrupt it.

Illegal wiretapping became a tool for repressing activists during the huge antiwar and civil rights movements in the 1960s and 1970s. FBI director Hoover acted as if the First and Fourth Amendments simply did not exist. It took Supreme Court cases—including *United States v. U.S. District Court*,[1] holding that President Nixon and his then–attorney general John Mitchell had no right to wiretap U.S. citizens in the United States without a warrant—to counter the government's suppression of Vietnam War protests. While that case concerned antiwar activities, subsequent revelations showed that Dr. Martin Luther King had been subjected to such warrantless wiretapping as well.

Almost 40 years later, after 9/11, President George W. Bush, contrary to that Supreme Court decision, claimed the right as president to engage in warrantless surveillance of citizens in the United States as part of his "War on Terror." Despite this action's clear illegality, no prosecution of Bush ensued, and Congress, including then-senator

Barack Obama, rather than condemning Bush's actions, formally granted the president the power he had illegally usurped, arguing that surveillance is a necessary tool to fight terrorism. It is not hard for government officials to find excuses for the curtailment of rights. Yesterday the pretext was anarchism or syndicalism or communism or the atom bomb or black liberation. Today it is terrorism.

In 1968 Congress was so concerned about mass protest that it enacted a statute that prohibited crossing state lines to incite a riot. Dubbed the Rap Brown Law after an African American leader who was its original target, the statute was applied by the government to the so-called Chicago 8, organizers of the protests at the Democratic Party's national convention in Chicago, which was the scene of a series of conflicts with demonstrators widely recognized to be the result of police overreaction. After a significant dormancy, the FBI invoked the law in October 2009 as legal justification for the search of the New York home of Pittsburgh G-20 demonstrators. Alleging violations of the law through use of the Internet, the FBI seized the computers in the house as well as artwork, correspondence with political prisoners, birth certificates, passports, videos, tax records, photographs, banners, posters, and flags.

REACTION AND COUNTERREACTION

In 1976, the Senate's Church Committee exposed the massive assault on dissent that the FBI, CIA, and other police agencies had perpetrated against opponents of segregation and the Vietnam War. This included keeping files on a million Americans, alleging that the NAACP was a communist front, and conducting burglaries of those being investigated. From the Church Committee hearings emerged restrictions on FBI spying activities and warrantless wiretapping and prohibitions on CIA operations in the United States. New guidelines for FBI domestic investigations were issued by the U.S. attorney general.

While by no means perfect, these first guidelines, named after Attorney General Edward Levi, limited surveillance of unpopular views, forbade monitoring of First Amendment activities absent a threat of violence, and permitted investigations only in the case of "specific and articulable facts" indicating criminal conduct. In the decades that followed, one attorney general after another weakened the guidelines, granting more and more authority to the FBI to engage in investigation of protected dissent in the United States.[2]

Even though the 1976 Levi guidelines represented the high-water mark of control of FBI attacks on dissent and protest, they were not particularly effective in preventing wide-ranging spying on and disruption of those opposed to U.S. intervention in Central America. The current slide toward a surveillance state originated with President Ronald Reagan's inauguration in 1981. The right-wing Heritage Foundation issued an influential report, "Mandate for Change," on the eve of Reagan's presidency calling for an unleashing of the FBI, the CIA, and the intelligence agencies. Reagan quickly followed with Executive Order (E.O.) 12333, broadening the authority of the intelligence agencies, particularly the CIA and FBI, to engage in intelligence and counterintelligence activities in the United States and abroad.

E.O. 12333, in conjunction with the Levi guidelines, made a distinction between allowable and unallowable government surveillance of U.S. organizations based on whether the organizations did or did not have any contact with foreign organizations or people. In order to monitor organizations without such foreign contact, the FBI had to show more evidence of potential or existing criminal conduct.

Central America was in turmoil throughout the 1980s, and those groups dissenting from U.S. policy in that region quickly became the focus of activities purportedly authorized by E.O. 12333. The Nicaraguan revolution had toppled Anastasio Somoza in 1979, El Salvadoran rebels under the umbrella of the FMLN were contesting power, and a strong insurgency was challenging the government in Guatemala. The Reagan administration decided to push back, creating and arming the contras in Nicaragua, supporting the government of El Salvador as it put down the rebels, and continuing military aid to the Guatemalan government as it violently repressed the insurgency.

Dissent against Reagan's policies in Central America, including mass public protests against intervention in the region, was a hallmark of the decade. Among other efforts to protect dissent in the 1980s, a "Movement Support Network" was set up by the Center for Constitutional Rights to monitor surveillance-type activities against protesters. The network received hundreds of complaints from activists about burglarized offices, FBI visits, possible informants, surveillance vehicles, and more. At around the same time, in March 1983, Reagan's first attorney general, William French Smith, issued new FBI guidelines authorizing spying under additional circumstances. Only an indication of possible wrongdoing, rather than any proof or even a "reasonable belief," became the new standard for surveillance, and a preliminary investigation could be opened with almost no evidence at all. As protest mounted, so did the authority to spy on and disable dissent.

In 1988, when documents requested under the Freedom of Information Act on behalf of the Committee in Solidarity with the People of El Salvador (CISPES) were released to the public, they revealed a vast government effort to surveil even the smallest antiwar groups, college campus organizations, and celebrities involved in antiwar activities. Efforts included the use of informers at many meetings and FBI visits to activists at their homes and places of work. Anyone returning from Central America drew special attention and surveillance. Often agents asked people they interrogated to continue to provide information—to become informants.

The FBI was doing the work of a political police, singling out key people and organizations dissenting from the government's policies, whether publicly or privately, and helping the administration to spy on and disrupt the opposition in the absence of any claim of criminality or violence. Much of the country was outraged. A major congressional hearing was held on the issue of spying, during which an FBI informant detailed his role in CISPES. (Today, in the post–9/11 world, it is unlikely that the revelation of such spying would engender much outrage, much less a congressional hearing.)

Despite the outcry over the revelations of spying on CISPES and other activists in the 1980s, surveillance of protest groups continued into the 1990s. Environmental groups such as Earth First! and Muslim organizations became new targets. The 1990s also saw the passage during the Clinton administration of the Antiterrorism and Effective Death Penalty Act of 1996, enacted in the wake of the Oklahoma City bombing. The act did not focus on that bombing but used it as a pretext to create a new category of prohibited activity: providing "material support" to any one of a list of organizations designated by the State Department as "Foreign Terrorist Organizations." These FTOs, including groups from countries as diverse as Palestine, Colombia, and the Philippines, have in common opposition to U.S. foreign policy. The "material support" law has been expanded since 9/11 to severely limit the rights of groups organizing against war and in favor of international human rights.

THE STATE OF DISSENT TODAY

The American government's crackdown on dissent became most pronounced and egregious in the wake of 9/11 and has taken both legislative and executive form—from the PATRIOT Act to the new FBI guidelines. New laws, rules, and regulations allow broad spying and surveillance by an FBI that can reasonably be described as a "political police," concurrent with severe limits on demonstrations, with bystanders, protesters, and journalists all subject to a level of arrest and detention previously unheard of in this country. Ethnic, religious, and racial profiling have grown rampant, and dissent often plays a factor in who is targeted. To be a Muslim activist, an environmental activist, or an antiwar protester in the twenty-first-century United States is to be a suspect. It is a dangerous time for dissent in America.

The PATRIOT Act and FBI Guidelines

In the aftermath of the 9/11 attacks, swift passage of the Bush administration's infamous USA PATRIOT Act was ensured, even though the act was a transparent attempt to use the excuse of antiterrorism to control criticism and protests of administration policies. Employing an absurdly broad definition of "domestic terrorism," the PATRIOT Act turns almost all forms of vigorous protest and minor criminal conduct into prosecutable acts of terrorism. For example, the act labels what would normally have been standard or Gandhi/King–like civil disobedience as domestic terrorism. Had the PATRIOT Act existed in 1999, protesters opposed to the World Trade Organization (see page 23) who technically engaged in trespass in demonstrating at the WTO conference in Seattle conceivably could have been charged with "domestic terrorism." But even passive protest—a march with a permit (which has become harder and harder to procure)—is no longer truly protected, with police on many occasions arresting marchers as a means of blunting the impact of a protest (specific examples are described throughout this section).

Examples of the misuse of domestic terrorism investigations against protesters were revealed in the 2010 report
by the Office of the Inspector General regarding the FBI's
investigations of domestic advocacy groups.[3] The report
examined five groups: the Merton Center (an antiwar
group), the Catholic Worker movement, PETA (People for
the Ethical Treatment of Animals), Greenpeace, and the
Quakers. The FBI investigations of these groups were initiated as domestic terrorism cases. The report states that
although these groups' activities would not "commonly
be considered terrorism," the practice of so classifying the
groups did not "violate the broad definitions of domestic terrorism in federal law, the Attorney General's guidelines, and FBI policies." The law permits just what activists
feared: domestic dissent is equated with terrorism. Such
investigations can have significant consequences for the
members of organizations so investigated, who are often
placed on watch lists, further investigated, and have their
travel tracked.

The PATRIOT Act granted the government remarkably
intrusive powers: to invade the privacy of Americans and
others living in this country, and to find out what individuals are saying, thinking, and doing. Broad new wiretapping provisions (which were evidently not broad enough
for President Bush, who consistently wiretapped outside
the minimal constraints of the new provisions) mean that
our conversations on the telephone and our e-mails are
not protected. The act also greatly expanded the availability of National Security Letters, which allow the FBI and
many other agencies to subpoena almost any personal information from a variety of institutions, including banks,

Internet service providers (ISPs), credit card companies, telephone companies, and even libraries. What is remarkable about National Security Letters is that the government can issue them without any judicial oversight, and the person about whom information is requested need not be a criminal suspect. Perhaps most frighteningly, the government can prohibit the institution from which information is demanded from informing the person about whom information is requested, or even from disclosing the fact that the institution has been served with a National Security Letter. Initially, the person about whom information is requested in such a National Security Letter could not even disclose its issuance to a lawyer. (After litigation, the statute has been amended and this restriction has been removed.) Hundreds of thousands of such letters have been issued since 9/11, with an average of around 50,000 per year.

The PATRIOT Act also broadened the "material support" statute and prohibited activities protected by the First Amendment. It redefined "material support" to include providing "expert advice or assistance." Even after passage of this amendment, many did not believe that the statute could legally prohibit educating groups about human rights laws. The Supreme Court said it did and could. In one of her final arguments before the Supreme Court as solicitor general, now–Supreme Court Justice Elena Kagan successfully argued for the extension of the definition of "material aid" to cover contacts with Foreign Terrorist Organizations, *including providing courses in peaceful dispute resolution*. The "material support" statute is becoming a favorite tool of the FBI and prosecutors pursuing those whose words and protests are critical of U.S. foreign policy.

Recent FBI raids on the homes and offices of numerous antiwar activists in Chicago and Minneapolis demonstrate the danger to dissent of the "material support" statute. In September 2010 the FBI and local police claiming to be seeking evidence of "material support" to FTOs in Palestine and Colombia—including FARC (Revolutionary Armed Forces of Colombia), Popular Front for the Liberation of Palestine (PFLP), and Hezbollah—executed search warrants demanding almost every shred of paper and electronic storage device in the places raided. The warrant makes for chilling reading and allowed seizure of "address books, lists, notes, photographs, videos, or letters of personal contacts in the United States and abroad." It authorized the taking of "computer equipment, electronic storage devices, and cellular telephones and their contents, including telephone numbers, photographs and videos." The danger to dissent is palpable: the government is misusing a dubious law to gather names and information about the activities of hundreds, perhaps thousands of political activists. Each of these persons will now be the subject of an FBI file and an investigation, if not more.

In addition to engendering the various new laws, the 9/11 backlash included the lifting of most of the remaining limits on the FBI contained in the earlier attorney general guidelines. The latest guidelines as of this writing, issued by Attorney General Michael Mukasey in the final months of George Bush's presidency, continue to govern FBI activities under President Obama and effectively allow and even encourage open hunting season on dissent in the

United States. These guidelines authorize FBI operations for law enforcement, national security, and foreign intelligence, effectively eradicating any limits on FBI spying in the United States, whether or not a person or group has a foreign connection. In addition, the guidelines permit the development of "terrorist profiles," openly putting forward a plan to make racial profiling official agency policy, continuing the systematic dismantling of constitutional protections. (The Mukasey guidelines are reprinted at the end of this book with an introduction describing them in more detail.) The Obama administration with the stroke of a pen could limit the broad powers given to the FBI under those guidelines. To date it has not done so.

The Return of COINTELPRO

The ghost of COINTELPRO has arisen in more ways than a renewed government effort at intensive surveillance of political activists. For example, in one case—that of the San Francisco 8—the old attacks on the Black Panther Party and the Black Liberation Movement, including police torture, have returned.

Under COINTELPRO's original campaign to neutralize political dissidents (primarily of the Left and anarchist temperaments), methods used to destabilize the Black Panther Party included spreading rumors regarding members' personal lives, putting snitch jackets on activists, publishing and planting false stories, conducting police raids and harassment, false arrests and charges, and murder. As of 1971, many of the BPP's leaders were either in prison, facing prison time, in exile, or murdered by the police. While

the FBI claimed to have ended its COINTELPRO activities in 1971, evidence presented in 1974 to the committee investigating the program's excesses proved otherwise.
Indeed, all that really occurred was that the program lost
its infamous name.

Two members of the San Francisco 8—Herman Bell
and Jalil Muntaqim—have been held for over thirty years
in New York State prisons on charges of murdering two
New York City police officers. Recently, old charges regarding the murder of a San Francisco police officer in
1971 were revived against them. The charges were first
thrown out in 1975, after the torture tactics of the police
were revealed.[4] (The torture faced by these men included
blindfolded beatings, being stripped naked and covered
in blankets soaked in boiling water, and the use of electrical prods on their genitals.)[5] In 2003, with funds ear-
marked by the Department of Homeland Security, the
case was reopened and the charges refiled, and in 2007
these veteran black activists were again accused of the
same crime, on the basis of the same old evidence pro-
cured by torture.[6]

The California attorney general's office stated that no
new scientific evidence had emerged in the case; on the
contrary, in the era of Guantánamo and extraordinary
rendition, the old torture evidence was all that existed. But
in an age of a new acceptance of torture, surveillance, and
the intimidation of activists, the Department of Homeland
Security and the California attorney general's office are
trying to resurrect evidence declared inadmissible thirty
years ago and set a dangerous precedent for the acceptance
of torture evidence produced by police agencies—not

only in Guantánamo's military commissions but in U.S. courts.

Seattle and Beyond:
Limits on Mass Protest

One of the dangers of the PATRIOT Act and the Bush guidelines for the FBI is that many people simply are not aware of the increased burden this complex of laws and practices places upon free expression. People who are unfortunate enough to be on a "no-fly" or watch list and find themselves harassed at airports are among those in the know. Sadly, another way to experience the effect of the new policing firsthand is to attend a demonstration or participate in its planning. According to Leslie Cagan, a longtime peace activist who headed United for Peace and Justice, new policing strategies "have greatly discouraged people from participating in demonstrations and certainly made parents think twice before taking their children."

The sea change in demonstration policing is generally traced to events in Seattle around the World Trade Organization Ministerial Conference in July 1999. In response to the negative impact of globalization on labor standards, fair trade, and environmental protection, prolabor and environmental groups organized their constituencies to protest at the conference. The most conservative estimates put the crowd at over 40,000, the largest demonstration at an international meeting in recent U.S. history.

Organizers formed a coalition called the Direct Action Network, with a public plan to "shut down" the conference. Through training in passive resistance and

nonviolent civil disobedience, the network's tactic was to
block downtown intersections to prevent delegates from
reaching the convention center. Blocking an intersection
is a well-worn labor and antiwar tactic, and during anti-
WTO demonstrations in Melbourne, Perth, Sydney, and
Darwin, these city centers were successfully blockaded.
On the morning of November 30, 1999, several hundred
activists blocked key intersections in Seattle and prevented delegates from getting from their hotels to the
convention center. The police cordon that had formed
around the center was cut off. Pepper spray, tear gas, stun
grenades, and rubber bullets were fired at protesters. As a
result, law enforcement agencies around the country were
concerned and embarrassed that the Seattle police proved
unprepared to deal with an event that had national and
international significance.

The first pictures released by the city and those most
repeatedly played by the media showed what was happen-
ing not downtown but rather a few blocks away, where a
small cadre of black-clad anarchists had begun to smash
storefront windows. Media coverage showing the smash-
ing of windows became the misleading visual signifier
of the Seattle protest. The police wanted to give the im-
pression that they were reacting to violence, but, in fact,
no violence was occurring downtown, where the police
employed repressive measures. False rumors of Molotov
cocktails and violent demonstrators circulated and further
served to blunt criticism of the police. Over 600 protesters
were arrested at the downtown demonstration and in its
aftermath.

Police officials across the country saw Seattle as their

Pearl Harbor. As a direct result, millions of dollars were spent on new riot gear, and police officials nationwide attended seminars sponsored by the National Association of Chiefs of Police and the U.S. Department of Justice to "provide public safety agencies with [the] skills, knowledge, strategies and tactics necessary" to control protesters.

The false rumors about the conduct of demonstrators persisted in order to justify the continued militarization of police. The *Boston Herald* in March 2000 reported that Seattle officers were briefing their Boston colleagues about their experience with crowds attacking police with "chunks of concrete, BB guns, wrist rockets and large-capacity squirt guns loaded with bleach and urine." In June, the *New York Times* reported that Seattle demonstrators had "hurled Molotov cocktails, rocks and excrement at delegates and police officers." (A subsequent *Times* correction said that Seattle protests were primarily peaceful, the only objects thrown were at property, and no protesters were accused of throwing objects, rocks, or Molotov cocktails at delegates or police.)

The formation of the Department of Homeland Security, the enactment of the PATRIOT Act, and the Bush administration's conflation of opposition to the Iraq war with support of terrorism combined to effect the most serious denigration of the right to dissent in many decades. Demonstrations—a staple of nonviolent protest during the 1960s and 1970s—became potential "civil disorders." Civil disobedience—a tactic at the heart of the civil rights movement—came within the new vernacular definition of "terrorism." In a message scarily reminiscent of McCarthy-era witch hunts, the Department of Homeland

Security warned local law enforcement in May 2003 to keep an eye on anyone who "expresses dislike of attitudes and decisions of the U.S. government."

In the wake of 9/11, the Departments of Justice and Homeland Security have poured almost a billion dollars into building up local and state police training, equipment, and intelligence-gathering efforts, creating more than 100 police intelligence units. Grants were originally made on the basis of "potential threat elements," but evolved into thousands of loosely defined targets, ranging from genuine terrorists to biker gangs and environmentalists. The Department of Homeland Security requires no verified evidence from its grantees for the alleged threat that the funding is meant to address.

In a telling reflection of today's "new policing" attitudes, law enforcement officials speaking in May 2010 at the fortieth annual commemoration of the Kent State antiwar protest (where National Guardsmen killed and wounded peacefully protesting students) surprised the crowd by failing to offer an apology for that infamous attack. Instead, the officials regaled the thousands who came to pay tribute to the students killed for their dissent with self-congratulatory statements, proudly trumpeting the technical advances the police had achieved in the intervening decades that now gave them the power to silence dissent with less-than-lethal force.

Comparing the events at Kent State with the 2009 Pittsburgh G-20 demonstrations, columnist John Mangels wrote in the *Cleveland Plain Dealer* that the National Guard had only steel helmets to "protect them from rocks thrown by protesters." He continued:

Flash forward to Pittsburgh in September 2009. Protesters at the G-20 economic summit were confronted by police imported from around the country and specially trained in crowd control by the Department of Homeland Security. Officers were armored with Kevlar vests and plastic shields, and cocooned in padded "turtle suits." Instead of bullets, they fired rubber rounds, bean bags and canisters of stinging pepper gas. Roving snatch squads whisked away individual agitators targeted by police surveillance. A "sound cannon" mounted atop an imposing black truck scattered protesters with painfully loud screeches and a booming, digitized voice that warned "YOU MUST LEAVE NOW!"

The equipment and tactics that officers use to control protests have changed dramatically in the decades since the Kent State tragedy. "We've come a long way in 40 years," said Charles "Sid" Heal, a recently retired Los Angeles County Sheriff's Department commander and veteran of numerous disturbances.[7]

The new policing poses a direct threat to the constitutional right to demonstrate. This new approach includes intelligence gathering and surveillance of protesters' preparations, manipulating media to paint participants as dangerous, disrupting planning through delayed permitting, scaring away participants through accusations of planned violence and civil disorder, displaying massive force and riot equipment, penning in crowds, cutting off marchers

with netting, tear gassing, shooting wooden or rubber bullets, tasering, playing sound machines, quick arrests, and
lengthy detentions.

Permitting and Privatization

Applying for permits to march or demonstrate—a key
component of protest and dissent—has become increasingly complicated throughout the country. Authorities
prolong discussions over routes, permitted sound equipment, and the very permissibility of the events. Organizers
get worn down and lose time to publicize mass protests. In
New York City, permit denial began early with the Giuliani
administration's refusal in 1999 to grant a permit for the
Million Youth March in Harlem, with the mayor labeling
it a "hate march." That event also witnessed the first use of
"penning" participants. With 6,000 participants and 3,000
police in attendance, some dubbed it "the Million Police
March."

The most egregious permit denial in New York City
occurred around the February 15, 2003, demonstration
organized by United for Peace and Justice to oppose the
looming invasion of Iraq. In denying protesters a permit
to march, the city took the position that the march posed
a unique security threat because terrorists might use it as
a cover to mount an attack. In the end, a stationary rally
was held on First Avenue, north of the United Nations
complex. Mounted police blocked streets and sidewalks
and prevented tens of thousands of people from reaching
the event. Those protesters who made it to First Avenue
were herded into overcrowded areas behind prefabricated

metal barricades. It was later learned that police interrogated many of those arrested at the rally and gathered information about political affiliations and past protest participation on a "Demonstrator Debriefing Form" that was entered into a computer database.

Some activists are convinced that by treating participants so badly, the Giuliani and Bloomberg administrations were effectively seeking the end of not only United for Peace and Justice but all mass demonstrations in New York City. Indeed, many activists subsequently determined that demonstrating was not worth the cost and looked for other ways to make themselves heard.

A year later, when the same group applied for a permit to hold a rally on the Great Lawn of Central Park the day before the start of the 2004 Republican National Convention, the city, with the support of the Central Park Conservancy, a private organization that raises money to support the park, denied the permit after many meetings and delays. Last-minute litigation was rejected by the courts.

Preemptive Policing

Preemptive policing, the domestic version of the doctrine of preemptive war, is just as pernicious as its international counterpart. It heralds a new paradigm of law enforcement that encourages police to rely on information about demonstration plans, organizers, and participants collected *in advance of events* to cancel protests and acts of dissent before any wrongdoing has occurred. Even assuming that such intelligence is reliable (most of the time police intelligence about protests is proven to be mistaken; the majority of demonstrators and bystanders arrested are found to be innocent of any crimes), the concept of relying on the ability of police to predict violations of the law flies in the face of the First Amendment. Well-established constitutional law prohibits the government in nearly all instances from exercising prior restraint of speech or association.

A major use of preemptive policing in the context of demonstrations occurred at the Republican National Convention in St. Paul, Minnesota, in 2008. For fifteen months prior to the convention, federal, state, and local agencies worked together collecting intelligence, planning, and taking preemptive steps to disrupt the event. The FBI set up an intelligence operation center and placed informants in protest groups in Iowa City and Texas. Although it's not clear whether this operation was a fusion center (one of more than 60 intelligence operations in which local police are joined by FBI agents to create computer systems that link with other agencies and data systems that mine and share information across the country), the Center for Investigative Reporting declared that a fusion center in Minnesota carried out "over 1,000 hours of support to intelligence operations" and "disseminated approximately 17 situation reports to over 1,300 recipients." Fusion centers in Iowa, Tennessee, Oregon, and South Dakota supplied Minnesota authorities with driver's license photos and criminal history records on people deemed suspicious in connection with the convention. Information was requested on where protesters were camping. It was suggested that photographs be taken of the protesters' belongings and where officers should seize supplies that might be used in "illegal direct actions."

The excuse for the heightened intelligence gathering was an amateur video showing youths dressed in black, their faces covered with bandannas, tossing homemade firebombs. No matter that the video was a parody, with the cocktail being used to light a barbecue grill and the bolt cutters used to cut a hedge; the video was the rationale for sending infiltrators to launch investigations into the RNC Welcoming Committee and other protest groups.

Other examples of preemptive policing include the following:

• **April 2000, Washington, D.C.**

Before demonstrations against the International Monetary Fund and World Bank were scheduled to begin, police chief Charles Ramsey claimed that police had discovered and raided a workshop for the manufacture of Molotov cocktails and homemade pepper spray at the activists' Convergence Center. DC police later admitted that no such workshop existed and what they had discovered was paint thinner used for art projects and peppers for cooking.

• **July 2000, Minneapolis**

Days before a protest against the International Society of Animal Geneticists, police falsely claimed that

activists had detonated a cyanide bomb. This false-
hood led to a raid on a house used by protest organizers, arrests of protest leaders, and seizure of materials.

• **August 2000, Philadelphia**

Hours before a protest against the Republican National Convention was to begin, police raided a
warehouse where protest organizers were preparing
banners and puppets, based on an alleged tip-off that
C4 explosives and water balloons of hydrochloric
acid were present. Even though nothing of the sort
was found, protest leaders were arrested and kept in
jail until the protests ended and the materials to be
used in the protest were destroyed.

• **Summer 2008, Maryland**

Maryland State Police entered the names and personal information of 53 peaceful left-wing activists
and protesters into state and federal databases and
identified them as terrorists. None of them had done
anything more violent than raising a placard against
the war in Iraq and the death penalty. They had been
investigated in 2005 and 2006. The state police super-
intendent who oversaw the spying told a state legislative hearing, "I don't believe the First Amendment
is any guarantee to those who wish to disrupt the
government."

Demonization

As mentioned earlier, a combination of the Seattle protest and 9/11 gave support to the scary conflation of demonstrators with terrorists. Mike van Winkle, the spokesperson for the California Antiterrorist Information Center, summed it up as follows: "You can make an easy kind of link that, if you have a protest group protesting a war where the cause that's being fought is against international terrorism, you might have a terrorist at that protest. You can almost argue that a protest against that is a terrorist act."

Examples of such demonization include:

- **2004, New York**

  One of the most concerted efforts at fear mongering occurred in New York before the 2004 Republican National Convention. One police official was quoted as citing "terrorist threats and the escalating plans of anarchist groups to disrupt the city of New York." Members of the press were invited to training drills. One mock protest showed people linking their arms inside metal pipes and storming a bus full of convention delegates. The *Daily News* reported on August 13 that "50 of the country's leading anarchists each accompanied by 50 followers" would be in town for the convention. A headline in the *New York Post* on August 16 read "Finest Prep for Anarchy." The article that followed included descriptions of three "high-profile, radical" anarchists. On August 20 the *New York Times* reported that police officials had "identified about 60 people as militants, some of whom were arrested for violent acts at past protests." On August 23, the *New York Post* quoted a top-level source as saying, "These people are trained in kidnapping techniques, bomb making and building improvised munitions." On August 31, ABC's *Nightline* displayed two dozen police intelligence photos of people termed by the police as "troublesome, even dangerous anarchists who infiltrate other groups of demonstrators and then try to provoke violence." Ted Koppel, the show's anchor, noted that some of the people had been under surveillance for 18 months. None were wanted for any crimes, and they were variously upset or amused by their characterizations. Brad Will, one of the people pictured, said he was planning to sue. A former East Village squatter and veteran activist, he was quoted as saying, "I never hurt anyone in my life. There are no cases pending against me. I am a journalist now. I don't want my career to be ruined. I don't want to lose my job." Will was subsequently shot and killed by Mexican authorities while filming demonstrations in Oaxaca in 2006. (One can't help wondering whether information about Brad Will was shared with Mexican authorities.)

• 2000, Philadelphia

The mayor of Philadelphia referred to the demonstrators who were planning to attend the 2000 Republican National Convention as "idiots." He warned, "Some will come here to disrupt, to make a spectacle of what's going on. They are going to get a very ugly response."

- **2003, Miami**

  Before the meeting of Western Hemisphere leaders at the Miami Summit of the Americas in 2003, circulars were distributed to local businessmen warning about the potential use of "Seattle tactics," including Molotov cocktails, crowbars, squirt guns filled with acid or urine, and wrist rockets or dangerous slingshots used to shoot steel ball bearings or large bolts. None of these weapons was used in Seattle or in any subsequent demonstration in the United States.

Crowd Control, Militarization, and Shows of Force

William Quigley, the legal director of the Center for Constitutional Rights, who has spent many years documenting the changes in forms of demonstration control by police, recently wrote, "Most big-city police departments have new armored vehicles and helicopters to fight terror. Every big police department has an antiterrorism squad now. At big protests it is now common to see local police dressed up like and acting like military commandos. This militarization of law enforcement clearly inhibits the free exercise of the First Amendment right to protest."[8]

Some recent examples of these tactics being put to use include:

- **2003, Oakland**

  At the antiwar demonstration at the port of Oakland
  in April, the Oakland police opened fire with wooden
  dowels, "sting balls," concussion grenades, and tear
  gas. Police fired into crowds to clear the street in front
  of the terminals. A city official who was there noted,
  "What happened today was very surprising. It seemed
  the police were operating under the assumption that
  they were not going to let any kind of protest happen.
  Local police were joined by FBI agents in the California terrorism information center. I've heard terrorism described as anything that is violent or has an
  economic impact and shutting down a port certainly
  would have some economic impact. Terrorism isn't
  just bombs going off and killing people."

- **2003, Miami**

  At the Miami protests against the Free Trade Act of
  the Americas, the police presence was overwhelming.
  Thousands of officers in military-style riot gear, in
  many cases with no identification, effectively swept
  the streets of all protesters and suspected protesters.
      Pursuant to a joint operational plan supported
  by Homeland Security, more than 40 states and local and federal agencies formed the so-called Miami
  Model of policing mass demonstrations in the United
  States. This consists of local/state/federal agencies
  collaboratively policing a protest, using a variety of
  dangerous "less-lethal" weapons against protesters,
  including batons, pepper spray, tear gas, and tasers.

333333

222222

• 2009, Pittsburgh

The G-20 Summit in Pittsburgh is a prime example of "command and control"—crowd management that severely limits demonstrations. First the police employ psychological attacks on the validity of the demonstrations with predictions of violence. In early August, the *Pittsburgh City Paper* reported on a Pittsburgh City Council hearing on the G-20 security situation. Addressing the council, Sam Rosenfeld, a former British army officer now heading the Texas-based security consulting firm Densus Group, advised the city to prepare for the protesters because they "want confrontation with police; in fact they don't care if an innocent person gets pulled in, because they know if it bleeds, it leads." He also warned about one of the groups involved in protest planning—the Pittsburgh Organizing Group—who, he predicted, would be attacking using "long poles from behind to stab at police officers . . . a la the Romans."

Police further deterred participation through the massing of its forces and the closing off of parts of the city designated "security zones" and "protest zones." A force of more than 6,000 officers descended on the city, including National Guards, Pittsburgh police, Pennsylvania state troopers, agents of the DEA, FBI, Homeland Security and Secret Service, private security firms, and police from New York, Maryland, Virginia, Illinois, Georgia, Michigan, and Kentucky.

On the morning of September 24, Pittsburgh was a ghost town: schools were closed as were most downtown businesses. Most government offices,

museums, and universities were shut. Public trans-
portation service was canceled in many areas, and
most downtown streets were closed to vehicle traffic. A security perimeter around the meeting spanned
a three-block radius, and almost every intersection
within two miles was guarded by armored personnel
carriers, police dogs, Humvees, mounted police, and
barricades or security fencing, as well as row upon
row of assorted law enforcement officers dressed in
riot gear. Numerous helicopters flew overhead.

"We tried very hard to create a sense that Pittsburgh did not have to shut down for the G-20 . . . but
I think the momentum was so strong that people just
decided to shut down," a Secret Service spokesman
explained (*Newsday*, September 21, 2009).

Only after a lawsuit was filed was a march permit
secured, just a week before the summit. The permit
was for a route well away from the closed "security perimeter," and the delay in securing it cut down on the
ability of organizers to publicize the march. Unper-
mitted marches were dispersed with tear gas, rubber
bullets, concussion grenades, and ear-piercing sirens
called Long Range Acoustical Devices (LRADs).

Political, social, and economic rights have only
been won in this country when they were demanded
in the streets. Historically, every administration in
power has viewed marches and mass demonstrations
as potentially destabilizing and has attempted to
prevent and disrupt them. Despite the indispensible
role of dissent and protest in bringing about critical
progressive changes on issues such as women's rights,

civil rights, gay and lesbian rights, and U.S. foreign policy, current government actions, laws, and regulations often treat these activities as crimes. Federal, state, and local law enforcers often label such dissenters terrorists and harass, detain, prosecute, and persecute them with impunity. We are quick to denounce the excesses of the McCarthy era in hindsight. But we are much slower to recognize the massive curtailment of First Amendment rights in our own day. We should be alarmed—and our alarm must be turned into action.

II.

IF AN AGENT KNOCKS

Federal law enforcement agencies like the Federal Bureau of Investigation (FBI) have a dark history of targeting radical and progressive movements. Some of the dirty tricks they use against these movements include: infiltration of organizations to discredit and disrupt their operations; campaigns of misinformation and false stories in the media; forgery of correspondence; fabrication of evidence; and the use of grand jury subpoenas to intimidate activists. Today's activist must know and understand the threat posed by federal law enforcement agents and their tactics as well as several key security practices that offer the best protection.

Federal agents have many tools at their disposal to target activists. While it is important to know and understand these tools and tactics, it is of critical importance that you resist any paranoia of government surveillance or fear of infiltration, which will only serve to paralyze you or your organization in your quest for social change. If fear of government repression prevents you from organizing, the agents of repression will have won without even trying.

VISITS AND SEARCHES

If I Am Approached or Called by a Law Enforcement Agent, Do I Have to Talk?

This is the most important piece of information to know: you have the right to remain silent, and it is usually the best idea to do so. The Fifth Amendment of the United States Constitution protects you from being forced to reveal self-incriminating information to law enforcement.

This is easier to say than to do. Agents are trained investigators: they have learned the power of persuasion and the ability to make a person feel scared, guilty, or impolite for refusing their requests for information. An agent may suggest that any unwillingness to speak with her/him means you must have something to hide. S/he may suggest s/he only wants you to answer a few questions and then s/he will leave you alone. The agent may threaten to get a warrant.

Don't be intimidated or manipulated by an agent's threats or assurances. It is always best not to talk without an attorney present. If you do talk, anything you say can be used against you and others. Even if you tell the whole truth, if the agent doesn't believe you, s/he can threaten to charge you with lying to a federal officer—which is a real crime.

Clearly convey your intention to remain silent. Say, "I'm not talking to you," or "I'd like to talk to my lawyer before I say anything to you." You can also say, "I have nothing to say to you. I will talk to my lawyer and have her/him contact you." You should ask the agent for a business card and say you will have your lawyer contact them. This should end the questioning.

The one exception to this rule is if you are in a state that has a "stop-and-identify" statute. All states require you to produce a driver's license if you are pulled over while driving an automobile, and the Supreme Court has held that laws that require you to state basic identifying information, such as your name and address, are not considered incriminating and that law enforcement may demand such information of you. They may only demand that information from you, however, if you are in a state that has a stop-and-identify statute. An activist attorney in your state should be able to tell you if your state has a stop-and-identify statute.[1]

The same basic rules apply if an agent calls on the phone. You do not have to speak to any agent who spontaneously calls you. Agents will often say that you are not part of any investigation. This may not be the truth. Tell anyone who identifies themselves as law enforcement that you will have your lawyer call them back—and then stop talking to them.

If possible, get the agent's name, telephone number, and agency. This should be on her/his business card, or s/he should be willing to provide this information. As soon as the agent leaves or hangs up, try to write down as many details about the interaction as you can. This information will be useful to a lawyer and to others who have been contacted by law enforcement. Try to write down the name of the agent(s) and her/his physical description; the type of car the agent was driving; the questions asked and comments made during the interaction; the date, time, and location of the encounter; and the contact information of any witnesses.

The best course of action is usually to get a lawyer involved. A lawyer can offer advice on how to proceed while protecting your rights. A lawyer can talk to the agent; find out what the investigation is about; try to set limitations on the subject matter of any questioning; and be present to advise and protect you if you are questioned. Sometimes a call from a lawyer is all it takes to get an agent to back off.

With the advice of a lawyer, you may consider publicizing the encounter to others who may be affected by an investigation. If activists know that there is an investigation, they can be more vigilant in protecting their rights. Organizing and public pressure can expose and limit intimidation and fishing expeditions.

What Are the Consequences If I Do Talk?

A situation may arise where you feel it is advisable to talk to an agent. Perhaps you have been the victim of a crime or you are a witness to civil rights violations being prosecuted by the federal government.

Even in those circumstances, you should have a lawyer present. A lawyer can make sure your rights are protected while you provide only necessary information relevant to a specific incident. They may be able to help you avoid a witness's appearance before a grand jury or control the circumstances of the appearance so that no one's rights are jeopardized.

If you do decide to answer questions, be aware that

lying to a government official is a crime. In fact, one of the most important reasons to not talk to an agent is this crime. A standard federal law enforcement tactic is to discover as much information as possible about a suspect or merely a person of interest to the government. Federal law enforcement agents will then approach that person at an otherwise ordinary time, such as during dinner or at the bus stop, and ask the person questions to which they already know the answers.

For example, an agent might ask if you know a person (whom they know that you know) or might ask if you were at an event (at which they know you were in attendance). If you instinctively say "No," that is a federal felony punishable with five to eight years in prison. The most daunting aspect of this investigative tactic is that many individuals will instinctively answer no to a question because they are scared or nervous. This tactic is used extensively by federal agents in all types of investigations and has been used recently to target and turn activists into informants against their former associates.

Lying to a federal officer is a federal offense and applies only to questions asked by federal agents. Be aware, however, that some local and state agents, such as members of a city's Joint Terrorism Task Force, are also considered "federal" agents. As well, some states have similar crimes regarding lying to a state officer. The safest choice is to not talk to law enforcement.

If you start answering questions, you can refuse to continue answering questions at any time.

Know Their Tools: Search Warrants

A search warrant is a court order authorizing law enforcement to search a specified location and seize evidence.

The Fourth Amendment protects people against unreasonable searches. Unless an exception applies, law enforcement agents are required to obtain a search warrant to conduct a search. Search warrants must be supported by probable cause, with facts sworn to by the officer applying for the warrant. A search warrant should be specific to the area to be searched and the object(s) to be searched for. It should be signed by a judge, be dated with a recent date (within a couple of weeks), and state the correct address for the location.

Probable cause means that facts must exist to establish that evidence of a crime will probably be found in the area to be searched. Probable cause must be based on facts—hunches are not enough.

Armed with a search warrant, law enforcement agents have the right to search your property. If you do not grant them access, they will likely use force to execute the search.

What If an Agent Asks to Search My Home, Apartment, or Office?

Never allow law enforcement to search your person or property without a warrant. Law enforcement agents are required to have a warrant to search your property except for certain limited circumstances. You are legally required to allow law enforcement agents into your home, office, or other private space only if they have a warrant.

Agents may search your house without a warrant if you allow them to, and they are trained to seek your consent to warrantless searches. Be careful of questions that are designed to elicit your consent to search. These questions may be as innocuous as "Do you mind if I come in?" Simply allowing an agent into your home may be construed as consent to search the whole place.

Legally, the best answer to a request to search is "I do not consent to a search." Say it loudly and proudly so any witnesses can hear.

What If I'm Not Around and an Agent Asks My Roommate to Search My Property?

A roommate can consent to a search of common, shared space and to her/his own space. A roommate cannot consent to a search of another person's private space in a shared house or apartment. In other words, a roommate could consent to a search of your kitchen, living room, or shared bathroom, but not your private bedroom, unless you share it with her/him or it is used as a common space in some way.

Spouses can consent to the search of their partner's private rooms because they are considered to have shared authority over all space in the house. Similarly, parents can consent to a search of their children's private space. In sum, if you share a bedroom with a roommate or partner, they can consent to a search of that space.

To protect against unwanted searches, make sure private space remains private. If you allow roommates to have mutual access and control over your private space, they can consent to a search of that space. Tell roommates, office mates, and anyone with whom you share space to never consent to searches of any space, especially your private space.

Can Agents Search My Trash?

Once you have placed your trash outside your house, agents can search it without a warrant or any other legal restraint. Courts have found that you have no privacy interest in your trash because you are surrendering it to the general public. Shred or otherwise destroy any and all sensitive documents before disposing of them.

What If an Agent Threatens to Get a Warrant or Grand Jury Subpoena Unless I Talk or Consent to a Search?

Don't be intimidated by an agent's threats to get a warrant or subpoena. This is one of the oldest tricks in the book. If it were so easy for the agent to get a warrant or subpoena, s/he wouldn't have wasted time trying to get your voluntary cooperation. Again, simply state that you will not consent to any search and that you will not talk without a lawyer present.

What If an Agent Claims to Have a Search Warrant?

If an agent claims to have a warrant, ask to see it. It must be signed by a judge to be valid. A search warrant should be specific as to the area to be searched and the object(s) to search for. Do not consent to an agent searching any areas not specifically included in a search warrant.

Just because an agent has a search warrant doesn't mean you have to answer any questions. Maintain your right to silence during the search—clearly state that intention if you are asked any questions.

What Rights Do I Have to Keep Agents from Searching My Car?

Law enforcement has extremely broad power to conduct warrantless searches of cars. If an agent has probable cause to believe that a car contains evidence of a crime, the agent may, without a warrant, search the vehicle and any container inside the vehicle that is large enough to contain the item for which s/he had probable cause to search. For example, if an agent has probable cause to believe you stole a large television, s/he can search the trunk of the car but not the glove box or a small toolbox in the trunk. If s/he has probable cause only to search a container recently placed in the car, s/he can search only that container.

If you are arrested and your car is impounded, law enforcement is allowed to perform a warrantless inventory search. This basically means the police may search your car for the purpose of cataloging what is inside, but they may use anything they find against you for any reason. Inventory searches must follow local established procedures, and the police may not use an inventory search as pretext for performing a warrantless search.

What Should I Do If My Office or Home Is Broken Into and I Suspect That the Motive Was Intelligence Gathering?

If your home or office is broken into, or if threats have been made against you, your organization, or someone you work with, share this information with everyone affected and take immediate steps to increase personal and office security. Contact a lawyer immediately.

Know Their Tools: "Sneak and Peek" Searches

"Sneak and peek" searches allow the government, with secret approval from a court, to conduct searches and surveillance without notifying the subject of the search. Since sneak-and-peek searches are intended to be carried out in secret, they usually are conducted through breaking and entering.

Normally an agent has to go before a judge and demonstrate probable cause in order to obtain a search warrant. In the Foreign Intelligence Surveillance Court, however, agents can obtain authorization to conduct a sneak-and-peek search if they can demonstrate that the search will provide foreign intelligence information. And foreign intelligence gathering doesn't have to be the primary reason for the search; it just has to be a significant reason for the search. This means that an agent can get authorization to search your home to gather evidence of criminal acts so long as foreign intelligence gathering is also a goal in the search.

While sneak-and-peek searches were designed for the purpose of gathering foreign intelligence information, most courts have allowed evidence and information obtained from sneak-and-peek searches to be used in criminal prosecutions.

Know Their Tools: Arrest Warrants

An arrest warrant is a court order authorizing law enforcement to arrest a specified person. Arrest warrants are signed and issued by a judge based on sworn applications from law enforcement attesting that there is probable cause that a crime has been committed and the person or people named in the warrant committed the crime.

In general, police and other law enforcement agents don't need a warrant to make an arrest. If they have probable cause to believe a crime has been committed, they can make an arrest.

There are two common exceptions to this rule. First, in most but not all states, law enforcement agents need a warrant to make an arrest for a misdemeanor that they did not witness personally. It is important to note, however, that agents can still make arrests for felonies they did not witness without an arrest warrant. Second, law enforcement generally needs an arrest warrant to make an arrest in your home. They can, however, make a warrantless arrest in your home if they believe there is a risk that you will destroy evidence or if they are chasing you in hot pursuit and you duck into your or someone else's home.

What Should I Do If Agents Show Up with an Arrest Warrant?

An arrest warrant is a tool used by police and other law enforcement agents to enter your home to make an arrest. One of the many loopholes in search warrant requirements is that once the agents are inside your home, even if they are there with only an arrest warrant, they have great leeway to conduct a search. They can search the immediate area around you without a search warrant. Law enforcement agents can even search the whole house as part

Know Their Tools: Subpoenas

A subpoena is an order issued by a government authority that demands someone turn over physical evidence, such as documents, or that the person testify in court.

Subpoenas are extremely easy to obtain. They are often filed by a government employee, a court clerk, and even private attorneys. A subpoena does not need to be presented to a judge before it is issued. The showing required to issue a subpoena is extremely low; a subpoena may be issued if there is any reasonable possibility that the physical evidence or testimony demanded will provide information relevant to the subject being investigated.

The ease with which subpoenas are issued makes them a powerful tool, but unlike search warrants or other government tools, they can be challenged in court prior to compliance. If you receive a subpoena, you can move to "quash" the subpoena if it is too broad or too burdensome or if it seeks legally protected materials, including materials protected by the First Amendment. Once a subpoena is quashed, the documents or testimony demanded are no longer required of the recipient.

Subpoenas are particularly dangerous because law enforcement can subpoena third parties that may have information about you. The government can subpoena other people for e-mails you have sent them. Or they can ask your e-mail provider for them. Because these third parties do not have the same interest in defeating these subpoenas that you do, they are more likely to comply with the subpoena without a fight.

of a "protective sweep" if they have a reasonable belief that a dangerous person might be present there.

If law enforcement arrives at your home (or any other space) with an arrest warrant, the best thing to do is go outside and give yourself up. If it is safe to do so, lock the door behind you. If law enforcement agents have an arrest warrant, they will arrest you. Do not give them the chance to conduct a warrantless search of your home as well.

What Should I Do If I Receive a Subpoena?

You should seek to quash the subpoena before the date of compliance specified on the subpoena itself, but even subpoenas that state they require immediate compliance cannot be enforced without a judge.

If someone shows up at your door and tries to serve you with a subpoena, just take it. Don't let the person in, don't answer any questions, and don't consent to a search. A subpoena does not give an agent the right to take any immediate action.

You should obtain the services of an attorney to help you quash the subpoena.

In the unlikely event that you are informed that a third party has been subpoenaed for records about you, you can move to quash that subpoena—it does not matter if a subpoena was issued directly to you.

INFILTRATION AND HUMAN SURVEILLANCE

The use of undercover agents and informants is indispensable in investigations by modern law enforcement agencies. The ability to place undercover agents or informants in progressive movements or organizations gives law enforcement a kind of access that is otherwise nearly impossible to obtain. Infiltration is very useful to collect

Know Their Tools: Informants

Informants are individuals who are not employed as law enforcement agents but provide law enforcement agents with information, often in exchange for money. An informant ordinarily has previous involvement in—and more intimate knowledge of—the movement or organization that the agents are investigating.

confidential information on the activities of private individuals and give law enforcement enough information to initiate an investigation. Undercover agents and informants can report to law enforcement on the participants, tactics, and actions of movements. They can even suggest, encourage, and/or participate in illegal activity in their efforts to arrest participants. Courts have generally held that public policy forbids the disclosure of an informant's name unless essential to the defense in a criminal court, so informants are rarely called upon to testify, enabling them to act with only a limited amount of responsibility or accountability.

Are There Limits on What Undercover Agents and Informants Can Do?

No specific law governs or limits law enforcement's use of undercover agents or informants, and there are no restraints on what types of crimes infiltration can be used to investigate. Unlike in other countries, the use of covert practices do not require a warrant, so law enforcement officers don't need to show that the use of an undercover agent or informant is necessary for a particular investigation.

The FBI's use of under-
cover agents and infor-
mants is governed only
by loose internal guide-
lines established after
U.S. congressional find-
ings in the *Final Report
of the Select Committee
to Study Government
Operations with Respect
to Intelligence Activities*
(1976).

The report exposed
details about the FBI's
now-infamous Coun-
terintelligence Program
(COINTELPRO), in op-
eration between 1956
and 1971, which tar-
geted activists and orga-
nizations, including Dr.
Martin Luther King Jr.
and the Black Panther
Party. In response to the
report, the U.S. attorney

Know Their Tools: Undercover Agents

An undercover agent is a law
enforcement officer who uses
an assumed name or fake identity to infiltrate a movement or
organization to gather information or evidence. In political
infiltration cases, an agent will
typically pose as a sympathizer
to a particular organization, gain
the trust of its key members, and
then use this access to gather
confidential information to pass
on to the investigative agency. A
secondary objective may be to
lay the groundwork for a separate
investigation. Undercover agents
typically concoct a cover story as
detailed as the assignment requires as well as a basic biogra-
phy and plausible story covering
past and present activities.

general enacted internal guidelines for covert FBI operations that regulated both undercover agents and informants. While these guidelines were initially strong, they
have been progressively weakened by several administrations. The current guidelines permit many of the invasive
law enforcement practices they were originally designed to

Know Their Tools: Cooperating Witnesses

Cooperating witnesses are similar to informants, except that cooperating witnesses usually agree to "flip" or "snitch" after being threatened with prosecution. Cooperating witnesses will testify in court in exchange for lesser charges being filed against them, if there are any charges filed against them at all.

Law enforcement recruits informants and cooperating witnesses from the ranks of people already active within the movements or organizations being targeted. The government often threatens these individuals with charges carrying massive jail time, offering to not file charges in exchange for a promise to inform on others in the movement. Undercover agents, on the other hand, use false pretenses from the beginning of their association with any movement or organization.

prevent. Moreover, the guidelines are not enforceable in court, so they offer only limited protection from infiltration and surveillance. In other words, if an agent gathers evidence in violation of FBI regulations, that evidence might still be used in court.

What Is Entrapment?

The strongest restraint on undercover agents and informants is the requirement to avoid entrapment. Entrapment occurs when an agent or informant plants the idea to commit an offense in the mind of an individual who would not otherwise have been disposed to commit such an offense and then encourages that individual to commit the offense in order to prosecute her/him. Courts view entrapment very narrowly, and tend to give wide latitude to undercover agents or informants who suggest or encourage illegal activity. While exceptions to the entrapment defense vary from state to state, it is generally not an effective defense if the undercover agent merely suggested the commission of a crime. In many states, entrapment is not a viable defense if a jury believes someone was predisposed to commit the crime. In other states, entrapment is not a defense at all when the crime involves "causing or threatening bodily harm." For these reasons, one cannot rely on the availability of an entrapment defense.

What Are the Constitutional Limits to an Agent's Power to Infiltrate?

Undercover agents or informants are generally allowed to attend public meetings, including those that take place in houses of worship. Courts have sometimes found First Amendment violations when it is determined that enforcement agents interfered with a group's ability to exercise the right to freedom of speech and association. Similarly, courts have found law enforcement in violation of the First Amendment when it gathers and publicly releases information on an activist or organization. Courts have not found First Amendment violations when law enforcement agents merely create an uncomfortable atmosphere at public meetings.

Courts have routinely found that the covert recording of conversations by undercover agents and informants does not violate the Fourth Amendment, which protects against unreasonable searches and seizures.

Courts have also found that the covert recording of conversations by undercover agents and informants does not violate the Fifth Amendment protection against self-incrimination. Similarly, if you unknowingly invite an undercover agent into your home or other private space, courts consider it "consent" to a search by that agent. If the undercover agent sees probable cause of a crime, s/he can then summon other law enforcement agents to join in the search based on the so-called consent granted to the undercover agent. Some courts have even applied the same reasoning for situations in which targets unknowingly invite an informant to enter a home.

How Can I Determine Evidence of Infiltration?

There are some helpful clues to identify an infiltrator. An undercover agent or informant may volunteer for tasks that provide access to your group's important meetings and papers, such as financial records, membership lists, minutes, and confidential files. Undercover agents and informants often encourage or urge the use of violence or illegal tactics and accuse others who resist those tactics as being cowards. Similarly, undercover agents or informants often accuse others of being agents or informants, thereby diverting attention from themselves and distracting the group from its work. An undercover agent or informant may also have no obvious source of income over a period of time or have more money available than her/his job should pay.

Try to obtain information on a suspected agent or informant's background. Check with organizations in areas the suspected agent lived in the past to see if anyone can vouch for her/him. See what you can turn up on the Internet. Public records such as credit reports, voter registration, and mortgages contain a wealth of information, including past and present addresses. If they are available, you might want to check listings of local police academy graduates, but remember that the suspected person may not be using her/his real name.

A person who fits these characterizations is not necessarily an undercover agent or informant. Use caution and do not accuse someone of being an agent or informant unless you have substantial evidence against them.

What Precautions Can I Take to Protect My Organization?

Maintain a file of all suspected or confirmed experiences of surveillance and disruption. Include the date; place; time; those present; a complete description of everything that happened; and any comments explaining the context of the experience and a description of the impact the event had on the individual or organization. Hold a meeting to discuss spying and harassment, and determine if any of your members have experienced any harassment or noticed any surveillance activities that appear to be directed at the organization's activities. Review past suspicious activities or difficulties in your group and try to determine if one or several people have been involved in many of these events.

You may try to file Freedom of Information Act (FOIA) requests for your organization from agencies such as the

FBI, Department of Homeland Security (DHS), the Bureau of Alcohol, Tobacco and Firearms, and other federal agencies. File similar requests with local and state law enforcement agencies utilizing your state's freedom of information laws. Most important, do not allow paranoia about infiltration to paralyze your movement or organization. Paranoia can be as destructive as infiltration itself.

ELECTRONIC SURVEILLANCE

This section addresses the ways that agents can use telephone wiretaps, bugs, and Internet surveillance in their investigations. As our lives become ever more digitized, agents are increasingly using electronic surveillance to collect information. Unfortunately, the law and the courts usually fail to keep up with the pace of technology, which often leads to unknown or diminished privacy protection for the latest technology.

A good rule of thumb is: the older the means of communication, the more protection the law affords it. As Eliot Spitzer said when he was New York State attorney general, "Never write when you can talk. Never talk when you can nod. And never put anything in an e-mail because it's death. You're giving prosecutors all the evidence we need."

Telephone Communications

Telephone conversations can be intercepted in a variety of ways—from taps to bugs to roving wiretaps to pen registers to trap and trace devices. Methods of telephone surveillance are detailed and complex and we can only offer an overview of them here. The lesson, however, is simple—be very careful about what you say on the telephone.

When Can the Government Tap My Phone Calls?

The government generally needs a special warrant called a Title III Wiretap Order to tap your phone. The government can, however, also tap your phone without a warrant for 48 hours under certain emergency situations involving immediate death or serious injury, national security, or activities characteristic of organized crime. The government can later seek a warrant to authorize continued surveillance that includes the prior wiretapping.

How Will I Know If My Phone Is Being Tapped?

Most likely, you will not know if your phone is tapped. Government surveillance has made great strides since the time when clicks, beeps, buzzing, or any other sound might tip you off to a tap. The government is generally supposed to tell you within 90 days after the surveillance ends, but notification can be postponed with relative ease.

What Is a Roving Wiretap?

Typically, a wiretap is applied to a specific phone at a specific location after it has been authorized through a court order. A roving wiretap, however, is a tap on any phone at any location from which the law enforcement

Know Their Tools:
Title III Wiretap Orders

Title III Wiretap Orders are the warrants that are used to intercept and monitor your communications. In addition to the Fourth Amendment protections requiring search warrants for most searches, Congress provided additional protections regarding oral communication in Title III of the Omnibus Crime Control and Safe Streets Act (1968). These increased protections were passed in response to the congressional findings of widespread illegal and abusive surveillance by the FBI in the 1960s (See "Are There Limits on What Undercover Agents and Informants Can Do?").

Agents must file a lengthy Title III application that includes: facts regarding the crime that has been or is about to be committed; the place from which communications will be intercepted; the communications sought to be intercepted; whether other investigative tools have been utilized and were inadequate or that other tools would be inadequate or too dangerous to apply; the time frame for interceptions to occur; and a statement on all previous wiretap applications concerning the same target or premises.

To issue a Title III Wiretap Order, a judge must find: probable cause that the target is committing a crime covered under Title III; that communication concerning that crime will be obtained by the interception; and that the facilities from which communication will be intercepted are being used in connection with the crime.

Originally, Title III permitted surveillance for only a narrow category of serious crimes. Over the years, Congress has added more and more crimes to Title III's coverage. Today, the law covers hundreds of crimes, including broad categories such as crimes involving drugs, riots, obscenity, or interference with commerce. Such broad interpretations of these crimes allow for the surveillance of many forms of activism.

Title III Wiretap Orders may initially last for up to 30 days. Law enforcement can return to the judge for repeated 30-day extensions. After a Title III Wiretap Order expires, the judge can order the government to disclose an inventory of intercepted communications to the targets of the wiretap. Such an inventory informs the targets of the time period of the wiretap and whether communications were actually intercepted. The judge may choose, however, to not require that such an inventory be issued.

Generally, it is a rare practice for law enforcement to seek wiretap orders, but they almost always get them when they ask. For example, in 2007, only 2,208 applications for wiretap orders were submitted to the state and federal courts, but every single application was granted in that year. The vast majority of the wiretap orders were in narcotics cases (1,792 out of 2,208, or 81 percent), with the next highest being homicide and assault cases (132 out of 2,208, or 6 percent).

agent believes the target will be making phone calls. Roving wiretaps have been allowed for government use since 1998. The government needs to meet the same standard for a roving wiretap as it does for a regular tap—probable cause that a crime has been or is about to be committed.

What About Bugs?

A bug is a miniature electronic device that can overhear, broadcast, and/or record a conversation. By placing a bug in your home or office, law enforcement can listen in on everything that is said within the device's range. The requirements governing the use of bugs are generally the same as those for wiretaps. The use of bugs presents some inherent difficulties for law enforcement agents: they must be installed within the target location; they are prone to malfunction; there is a risk of discovery; and they may be rendered useless by electrical interference. Because of these difficulties, bugs are likely used to a lesser degree than wiretaps.

Know Their Tools: Pen Registers and "Trap and Trace" Devices

A pen register device records the numbers dialed from a telephone line to which the device is attached. "Trap and trace" devices record the telephone numbers of incoming calls.

A court order is required if law enforcement wants to install and use either device; however, these court orders are very easy to obtain. The government needs only to believe that the information likely to be obtained is relevant to an ongoing criminal investigation. Judges and law enforcement typically take a very broad view of what is likely to be relevant to an investigation. Many states allow such surveillance under even more lax standards. Also, the U.S. attorney general can, in certain "emergency" situations, authorize the use of these devices for up to seven days without seeking an order from the judge.

The PATRIOT Act expanded the permitted use of both pen registers and trap and trace devices. Some expanded uses of pen registers and trap and trace devices include: tracking the physical location of cell phone users; recording the addresses of Web sites you visit; the Internet protocol (IP) addresses that your computer connects to; or the IP addresses of computers that connect to your computer. An IP address is a unique number assigned to each computer or device that connects to a network.

What About the Foreign Intelligence Surveillance Court and the National Security Agency's Warrantless Wiretapping Program?

The government can wiretap both citizens and noncitizens if there is probable cause to believe that the target is a member of a foreign terrorist group or an agent of a foreign power. In order to wiretap citizens and lawful permanent residents, the government must also demonstrate probable cause that the target is engaged in activities that "may" involve a criminal violation. For this type of surveillance, the government must obtain a search warrant from the Foreign Intelligence Surveillance Court, a secret court in which hearings and records are closed to the public. The government, via the National Security Agency (NSA), claims the authority to warrantlessly monitor any telephone or electronic communication if it believes one party is located outside of the United States—even if the other party is inside the United States. While the NSA is authorized only to monitor communications for purposes of obtaining foreign intelligence, the full scope of the program is unknown.

What Security Threats Do Cellular Phones, Smartphones, and PDAs Pose?

The convenience and ease of cell phone communication comes with significant privacy and security risks. Be aware of the risks inherent in using these devices and weigh the convenience benefit to the security risk before each cell phone use.

The same legal rules that apply to landlines apply to getting a tap, pen register, or trap and trace device on a cell phone. It is important to note, however, that anyone with a few hundred dollars' worth of equipment can intercept your cell phone signals. And you shouldn't assume that agents always follow the law. Individuals and corporations may also easily intercept your cell phone signals with little risk of being caught.

The government has the ability to turn a cell phone into a listening device or a "roving bug." This allows the government to hear any conversations that take place near the cell phone. The government does not need access to the cell phone itself to "plant" a roving bug, but can simply initiate it through your cell phone company. Roving bugs allow the government to hear conversations near your cell phone even when it is turned off. It appears, however, that physically removing the battery from a cell phone will disable a roving bug.

Your cell phone can also be used to track your location. Whenever your cell phone is on and has a signal, it is in contact with one or more cellular towers in your area. The government can monitor these connections to determine your physical location. In cities and other areas with a higher density of cellular towers, your location can be tracked more precisely, sometimes within a few yards. Currently, there is no uniform legal standard for this kind of cell phone tracking. Some courts require agents to meet the same low showing needed to obtain a pen register or trap and trace device, while other courts require agents to obtain a warrant supported by probable cause. The government can also go through your past cell phone records to determine your location at that time if your cell phone was turned on.

Some courts have held that once you are arrested, law enforcement can, with a warrant, search the call history and contacts stored in your cell phone. Some courts have even held that, after a lawful arrest, law enforcement can search text messages, pictures, e-mails, and any other records contained on your phone. Some courts allow law enforcement to search call histories without a warrant, with the argument that the call history will yield the same information that can be obtained by a pen register, but require a warrant for searching text messages or e-mails. The courts are still developing this area of law; as a result, laws and regulations vary from jurisdiction to jurisdiction. Enabling password protection on your cell phone offers some level of protection against the security risks inherent in cell phone usage.

Can the Government Monitor My Text Messages?

Text messaging is a considerably insecure method of communication. Like cell phone conversations, text messages can be easily intercepted by anyone with the right equipment. Neither Congress nor the courts has been clear about whether probable cause and a warrant are required to intercept text messages, so law enforcement may attempt to intercept text messages using pen registers or trap and trace orders, which are relatively easy to obtain. Finally, because text messages are not considered "wire communications," they are not protected by the exclusionary rule of the Wiretap Act. So even if the government illegally intercepts your text messages, it can still use these communications against you in a criminal trial.

INTERNET COMMUNICATIONS

Law enforcement can easily access much of your electronic communications and the information they contain.

Can the Government Read My E-mail?

To obtain a subpoena to access your electronic communications, the government needs only to demonstrate that the information likely to be obtained is relevant to an ongoing criminal investigation. With the subpoena, the government can obtain your "basic subscriber information," which includes the name and physical address associated with an account; the length and types of service used; session logs; and the IP address of your computer.

The government needs a D Order (see "Know Their Tools: D Orders") to obtain other "noncontent records," which include any records or logs that reflect the e-mail addresses you send e-mail to or receive e-mail from; times and dates on which e-mails were sent or received; and the size of each e-mail.

Regarding e-mail stored by a third party, such as a Web e-mail service or an Internet Service Provider (ISP), different protections apply depending on how recent an e-mail is and whether or not you have read it. The Stored Communications Act requires law enforcement to obtain a search warrant for the content (subject line and body) of unopened e-mails that have been in storage for less than 180 days. For unopened e-mails older than 180 days and for opened e-mails in storage by the third party, the government can obtain a D Order or issue a subpoena for the content of the e-mails. The government can also choose to get a search warrant for e-mails older than 180 days or for opened e-mails.

In Alaska, Arizona, California, Hawaii, Idaho, Montana, Nevada, Oregon, and Washington, which are states covered by the Ninth Circuit Court of Appeals, courts have disagreed with the government's interpretation that it can, with a D Order, obtain opened e-mails that have been in storage for less than 180 days. These courts have ruled that the government needs a warrant for any e-mail that is less than 180 days old.

Know Their Tools: "D Orders"

Another law enforcement tool is the 2307(D) Order, commonly referred to as a "D Order." The D Order gets its name from the subsection of the Stored Communications Act that authorizes it. The government uses D Orders to obtain electronic records stored by third parties—most often, e-mail. D Orders are harder to get than a simple subpoena but easier to obtain than a search warrant. To obtain a D Order, the government must provide specific facts to a judge showing there are reasonable grounds to believe the information sought is relevant to an ongoing criminal investigation. So the suspicion required for the D Order is lower than probable cause, but it is higher than the standard of "any reasonable possibility" required in order to obtain a subpoena.

The government is supposed to give the individual

subscriber prior notice before using D Orders or subpoenas to obtain the content of e-mail. In theory this would allow the subscriber to move to quash the subpoena before the third party complies with it. Another provision of the Stored Communications Act, however, allows law enforcement to delay notice of a D Order or subpoena for a substantial period of time, and it appears the government regularly delays notice. Law enforcement can also avoid giving you any notice by taking the extra steps required for a search warrant.

Larger ISPs reportedly receive more than 1,000 subpoenas each month seeking information about their users. Most of the subpoenas request users' names, addresses, ISP addresses, and records of when the target signed on and off of the Internet.

There are many reports of law enforcement programs designed to capture vast amounts of Internet traffic, including e-mails and Web activity. The extent of these programs, their permitted use, and the admissibility of any information obtained through them in court is currently unknown.

Can the Government Tell What Web Sites I Visit?

Law enforcement needs a warrant for records of the actual Web sites you visit. The government can reportedly obtain the uniform resource locator (URL) addresses—e.g., http://ccrjustice.org—of Web sites you viewed without a warrant, but the government needs a warrant to obtain information on specific pages you visit on a Web site, e.g., http://ccrjustice.org/ifanagentknocks.

Should I Be Wary of Electronic Surveillance from Nongovernmental Entities?

Corporate spying is likely a larger industry than government spying. Corporations routinely hire private spies, most of whom are former law enforcement agents, to conduct surveillance of activists who may threaten their interests. Corporate spying involves many of the same tactics employed by the government, including: rummaging through trash; tapping telephones; monitoring Internet activity; and using infiltrators. Corporate spies are probably less likely to be concerned by legal restraints on spying.

Know Their Tools: National Security Letters

The National Security Letter (NSL) is a tool used by the FBI to secretly demand information about an individual from a third party, such as a telephone company, ISP, consumer credit agency, or financial institution. NSLs require no probable cause or oversight—the FBI needs only to believe the information it seeks is relevant to a terrorism or espionage investigation. The NSL law has a built-in gag rule that prohibits someone who receives an NSL from telling anyone except their attorney that they have received one. Though a recent court ruling found the permanent, built-in gag rule unconstitutional, its future application remains unclear.

Government studies have reported that the FBI issues tens of thousands of NSLs a year, and often violates even the minor restraints on its authority to issue these letters. Data from NSLs is shared within the U.S. intelligence community, other government agencies, and even foreign governments.

If you or an organization you work with receives an NSL, contact an attorney immediately.

Know Their Tools: Electronic Security

Electronic security is an immense and complex topic. This section introduces some basic advice regarding electronic security. Simply put, the most secure electronic communication is no electronic communication at all. Effective electronic security habits require maintaining a constant balance between the convenience and the risks associated with electronic communication. As with any practice, you should weigh risks against rewards when deciding what electronic security measures to employ.

DATA ENCRYPTION

Encryption is a method of turning information into a ciphered code. If used properly, encryption protects your data from being viewed by anyone who does not have the proper "key" to view it. Modern encryption technology is strong enough so that it is virtually impossible for the government to unscramble encrypted messages without the use of keys. Encryption is the strongest protection you have to prevent the government from obtaining your electronic data.

Widely available programs allow you to encrypt all of the data on your hard drive. Simple passwords to log in to your computer are not enough to protect your hard drive. The government can take the hard drive, make a copy of it, and easily access the data without your login. With an encrypted hard drive, your files will be encoded and the government will not be able to access them without your encryption password.

Encryption programs also allow for encryption of individual files or folders. While this may be easier to manage, piecemeal encryption may allow for additional vulnerabilities to those files. A better solution is to keep a separate, fully encrypted hard drive for sensitive files.

E-MAIL ENCRYPTION

Using encryption is even more important for e-mail. We've already shown how the government can use D Orders or subpoenas to easily access your e-mails or use other tools to intercept them in transmission. And once an e-mail is on a third party's computer, you have no control over who can get it and read it. Similar to data encryption, one tool to protect your electronic communications is e-mail encryption. In order to use e-mail encryption effectively, however, both you and whoever you are communicating with must use an encryption program.

E-mail encryption ensures that only the intended recipients can read the e-mail you send. Modern e-mail encryption works through a system of "public keys." A public key provides instructions, or the code, for how e-mails sent to you should be scrambled. The code to unscramble messages—the "private key"—is different from the public key, and only you have access to the private key. If your e-mails are intercepted through a subpoena, court order, or otherwise, the messages contained therein cannot be unscrambled without your private key.

While the more technical aspects of e-mail encryption are too detailed to include here a simple analogy to encryption is an open door that can be locked by anyone but can be opened only by someone with a special key.

E-mail encryption is easier to use today than it was in the past. GNU Privacy Guard (GnuPG) is a free program that can be integrated into most major e-mail programs. For example, the third-party mail client Mozilla Thunderbird offers a plug-in, also known as a security extension, called Enigmail that is compatible with GnuPG and makes encryption fairly easy to use.

PASSWORDS

Take passwords seriously. Don't use a word or a word with a number at the end or in the middle. Those passwords can be easily broken

(continued)

after a few attempts. Use a series of characters that make sense only to you.

Don't use the same password twice for any account that has private information. Try to keep your passwords in your head. Written passwords can be discovered or subpoenaed. Change your passwords every couple of months. If you do write your passwords down, try to write them in a code only you understand. If you decide to write down a password, never leave it next to or near your computer; you're better off keeping them in your wallet.

Consider using a "password safe" program. These programs allow you to keep your passwords in a single encrypted file on your computer so you need to memorize only one password to access all your other passwords. Do not write your master password down, since it is the password that protects all others.

WEB BROWSING

Carefully manage the data that your Web browser may keep regarding your Internet activity and the data that other Web sites may have about you.

As a default, Internet browsers keep a great deal of potentially private information, including but not limited to: the Web sites you visit; passwords for those Web sites; and even images from the Web pages you visit. An agent who gets hold of your hard drive can learn a lot about your Internet activity from these files. Delete this information regularly. Set your browser to delete your Internet browsing history, cache, cookies, download history, saved forms, and saved passwords regularly. You may want to do this daily or whenever you close your browser.

Whenever available, use a Web site's built-in encryption when browsing to prevent third parties from intercepting the information transmitted. Web sites that have built-in encryption start with https:// instead of http://. Consider using anonymous Internet tools such as Tor. Tor is an encryption and anonymization program that routes your data only through other Tor clients, encrypting your data along the way and stripping out information regarding where the data originated. Each Tor router knows only the address of the last router it went through, making it extremely difficult to trace any communication back to its original source. Some drawbacks to using Tor are slower speeds at which Web pages load, and many unsecured functions such as Flash do not work over Tor.

KNOW YOUR INTERNET SERVICE PROVIDERS

Read the terms of service and the privacy policies of any electronic service you are considering signing up for. Some ISPs, including several that are tailored to the needs of political activists, provide stronger privacy protections and claim to be more resistant to government snooping.

USE ANTISPYWARE PROGRAMS

Purchase a good antispyware and/or antivirus program and regularly update them. Spyware can breach all of your electronic security, logging every Web site you visit and every keystroke on your machine. Major antispyware companies claim they treat government spyware the same as any other spyware.

DATA RETENTION AND DELETION

The government can't get what doesn't exist. Establish a data retention policy in which you review and delete old files on a consistent basis. Do not selectively destroy documents—pick a time frame and stick to it. You can establish a different schedule for different types of data, e.g., delete computer files every two months; delete e-mails every two weeks; and delete Web browser logs every two days. Whatever the policy is, stick with it. After all, do you really need the last three years of e-mails?

Do not destroy anything that has been subpoenaed—if you do so, you run the serious risk of an obstruction of justice charge. Keep a written record of your data retention policy to protect yourself and your organization against accusations of destroying evidence.

GRAND JURIES AND GRAND JURY RESISTANCE

What Are Grand Juries and What Threats Do They Pose to Activists?

A grand jury is a panel of citizens brought together to investigate crimes and issue indictments. In their original conception, grand juries were intended to be radically democratic. In England, they served as a buffer between citizens and the monarch and her/his prosecutors. In early America, any citizen could bring an allegation of wrongdoing to the original grand jury and the grand jury could indict on a majority vote.

Modern-day grand juries are very different. Today, all cases are brought to a grand jury by a prosecutor. The prosecutor picks the witnesses and asks the questions. Witnesses are not allowed to have a lawyer present. There is no judge present. The prosecutor drafts the charges and reads them to the grand jury. There is no requirement that the grand jury members be instructed on the law at issue. And, unlike in other juries, grand jury members are not screened for bias.

Since the prosecutor solely orchestrates the proceedings, it is no surprise that grand juries almost always serve as a rubber stamp for prosecution. A former chief judge of New York once famously noted that "any prosecutor that wanted to could indict a ham sandwich." In the rare event that a grand jury does not indict, the prosecutor can simply impanel a different grand jury and seek an indictment before a new grand jury.

In political cases, grand juries have been used to execute

witch hunts against activists. Prosecutors will bring in activist witnesses and attempt to get them to snitch on other activists with threats of jail time if they refuse to cooperate with the grand jury. It is critical to understand how a grand jury works; what your rights are; what rights you cannot exercise; and how to resist a grand jury.

Many rights we take for granted do not exist for grand jury witnesses. Grand jury witnesses have no right to be represented by an attorney and no right to a jury trial if they are threatened with jail. Grand jury witnesses do retain the right against self-incrimination, but can nonetheless be forced to snitch on themselves and others in exchange for immunity from prosecution and punishment. Immunity protects only witnesses—others can still be prosecuted.

What Should I Do If Someone Shows Up with a Grand Jury Subpoena?

Grand jury subpoenas are served by law enforcement agents, usually police officers or federal marshals. A grand jury subpoena must be personally served on you, meaning, it must be handed to you. If you refuse to accept it, it must be placed near you.

A grand jury subpoena does not give an agent the right to search a home, office, car, or anywhere else, nor does it require you to relinquish any documents or say anything at that time. A grand jury subpoena only requires you to do something on the future date stated on the subpoena.

If an agent shows up and tries to serve you with a subpoena, take it and do not do anything else. Do not answer any questions; do not consent to a search; and do not invite the agent into your home for any reason.

What Options Do I Have If I Receive a Grand Jury Subpoena?

Once you have received a grand jury subpoena, you typically have three options: (1) You can comply with the subpoena; (2) you can move to quash the subpoena; or (3) you can refuse to comply. If you receive a subpoena, you should contact an attorney as soon as possible

Know Their Tools: Grand Jury Subpoenas

Grand juries get information from people by issuing subpoenas. A grand jury subpoena is an order to testify before a grand jury or provide the grand jury with certain information. Grand juries issue different types of subpoenas for testimony and information. A *subpoena ad testificandum*, or testifying, is a subpoena ordering a witness to appear and give testimony. A *subpoena duces tecum*, which means "bring it with you" in Latin, is a subpoena ordering a witness to provide the grand jury with certain documents. Grand juries also use these orders to obtain fingerprints and handwriting samples. Grand juries often issue both subpoenas to the same witness so they can obtain both documents and testimony.

and discuss each of these options in detail.

Complying with a subpoena is relatively straightforward. For a *subpoena ad testificandum*, you arrive at the date, time, and location stated on the subpoena and answer the prosecutor's questions. For a *subpoena duces tecum*, you show up on the date, time, and location stated on the subpoena with the documents or other evidence required.

If you comply with a subpoena, you avoid the possibility of being punished for ignoring it; however, complying with a subpoena may get you into a different type of trouble. For example, if you are a target of the investigation, complying with the subpoena may provide the government with information it might need to charge and convict you. You might also place another activist in jeopardy by complying with a subpoena.

If you receive a subpoena, you should speak with a lawyer before taking any action. If the subpoena is politically motivated, it is best to speak with an attorney in your activist circle who does criminal defense or grand jury work. Some nonactivist criminal defense attorneys may suggest you become a snitch. It is important to note, however, that many snitches end up serving as many years in prison as the individuals on whom they snitched.

Grand jury proceedings are secret. The activist community often does not know when a grand jury investigation is being pursued. As a result, many activists believe that they should publicize the fact that they have received a subpoena. This may be an effective tactic to explore with your attorney if you receive a subpoena.

How Do I Quash a Grand Jury Subpoena?

You can challenge a subpoena in court by a motion to quash the subpoena. Quashing a subpoena means a court declares it null and void. A court will grant a motion to quash only if there is a sufficient legal basis, such as misidentification; lack of jurisdiction; a protected privilege; or an unlawful basis of the proceedings.

Even if you cannot successfully quash a subpoena, litigating a motion to quash in court can buy you some time. Time is important, especially if you do not plan to cooperate with the grand jury, because noncooperation can land you in jail. Grand juries can last for as long as 18 months; whatever time is spent litigating the motion to quash may save you the experience of spending that entire period in jail.

While there is little to lose by filing a motion to quash a *subpoena duces tecum*, the subpoenas that demand evidence, motions to quash *subpoenas ad testificandum*, which demand testimony, can present problems. At least one federal circuit court ruled that you lose any objections that were not raised in the original motion to quash. You should not waive your objections, especially because you may not know what your objections are until you are asked a particular question.

A good political attorney should be able to provide advice on whether moving to quash a subpoena is a good idea or not in your particular circumstances.

What Happens If I Refuse to Comply with a Grand Jury Subpoena?

There are two basic ways to refuse to comply with a grand jury subpoena: (1) refuse to show up; and (2) refuse to answer any of the prosecutor's questions.

If you simply refuse to show up for your testimony, you may be in contempt and the government can choose to arrest you and jail you until you testify or until the grand jury expires. If your testimony is not particularly important to the prosecutor, they may choose not to take action.

What Happens If I Comply with a Grand Jury Subpoena?

If you appear to testify, you will not be allowed to have an attorney present. You can, however, have an attorney just outside the grand jury room, and you can consult with her/him after every question, although some courts have ruled you can only consult your attorney after every few questions.

Because you retain your Fifth Amendment right against self-incrimination, you can refuse to answer the prosecutor's questions by saying "I invoke my Fifth Amendment privilege against self-incrimination" after every question. At this point, the prosecutor may simply dismiss you or s/he may seek to grant you immunity.

Immunity prevents the witness from having criminal charges brought on the basis of the grand jury testimony. A judge must approve a grant of immunity. A prosecutor can get a judge to preapprove a grant of immunity; otherwise, a witness is brought before a judge who, upon the prosecutor's request, virtually always grants immunity.

If you continue to refuse to answer questions after being granted immunity, the prosecutor can bring you before a judge, and the judge will order you to testify. If you continue to refuse, the judge can have you jailed for civil contempt. Witnesses who refuse to provide physical exemplars—i.e., samples of handwriting, hair, appearance in a lineup, or documents—upon the request of a grand jury may also be jailed for civil contempt.

While civil contempt is not a crime, it can result in the witness being jailed for the duration of the grand jury. Grand juries can last for up to 18 months, although some "special" grand juries can obtain up to three extensions of six months each. The purpose of incarcerating a recalcitrant witness is to coerce her/him to testify. Judges will sometimes free witnesses before the expiration of the jury if it is clear that there is no chance the witness will testify.

The government can also use the charge of "criminal contempt" against uncooperative grand jury witnesses. Criminal contempt carries no maximum penalty—the sentence depends entirely on the judge's discretion. While civil contempt is meant to coerce a witness to testify, criminal contempt is meant to punish a witness for impeding the legal process. As with any other crime, criminal contempt requires notice of the charges, the right to receive assistance of counsel, and proof beyond a reasonable doubt. Charges of criminal contempt are extremely rare.

If you are jailed, you can periodically file a motion stating that: (1) jail will not coerce you into testifying; and (2) your confinement is merely punitive and therefore unconstitutional. If you win one of these motions, you will be released.

Some activists create files to prepare for being called before a grand jury. A file that memorializes your stalwart belief against cooperating with grand jury proceedings can be used as evidence that civil contempt will not work to coerce you and thereby help you win release.

What Happens After a Grand Jury?

What takes place in grand jury proceedings is secret. The government relies on this secrecy to create fear and distrust in activist communities. Some activists have successfully dispelled that fear and distrust in their communities by publishing the questions asked of them by the prosecutor and the answers they provided. If you are considering taking action in this way, you must talk with an attorney to ensure that you are not creating more problems than you are solving.

SPECIAL CONSIDERATIONS FOR NONCITIZENS

Noncitizens are individuals who do not have U.S. citizenship, including tourists, students, and others who are in the United States on visas or visa waiver programs; lawful permanent residents; refugees; and those without legal immigration status. Noncitizens in the United States share most of the same constitutional rights as citizens. There are some exceptions to that rule, and noncitizens engaging in political activism should be aware of several special considerations. Noncitizens should not, however, entirely avoid political activism based on an unreasonable fear of government repression.

Speech and Political Affiliations

In most cases, the government treats speech by noncitizens in the same way it treats speech by citizens. Noncitizens cannot be criminally punished for speech that would be protected if uttered by a citizen. Similarly, noncitizens cannot be sued for speech that would be protected if said by a citizen.

The government does, however, have broad powers to withhold immigration benefits (such as discretionary relief or naturalization) and may potentially even initiate removal proceedings based on a noncitizen's speech. It is unclear whether the government can remove a noncitizen or withhold discretionary benefits for speech or political association alone. Fifty years ago, some courts found the government could, but First Amendment law has changed dramatically since then, and courts are now split on whether that rule is still good law. Practically speaking, it is extremely rare for the government to remove someone based purely on speech or association. However, the government is allowed to selectively enforce immigration laws. For instance, the government can remove noncitizens for violations of immigration law (such as overstaying a visa or working without authorization) even if the government's motivation in initiating removal proceedings is a noncitizen's speech or political association.

Finally, applicants for permanent residence and naturalization are asked to list the organizations with which they have worked. Politically active noncitizens are advised to consult an immigration lawyer before applying for a change in status because some associations may cause problems in your application process.

Searches and Seizures

Noncitizens largely enjoy the same Fourth Amendment protections against unreasonable searches and seizures that citizens do. Law enforcement must get a warrant to perform any search on a noncitizen or a noncitizen's property just as they must to perform a search on a citizen. Evidence obtained in violation of the Fourth Amendment is excluded from a noncitizen's criminal trial the same way it is for citizens.

Unfortunately, the use of evidence obtained in violation of the Fourth Amendment is generally permissible in immigration proceedings. This means the government can use illegally obtained evidence that cannot be used in criminal proceedings for immigration proceedings. It is possible that evidence obtained through especially egregious violations of the Fourth Amendment may be excluded in immigration proceedings.

Also, the government can generally search and seize any person, package, or vehicle traveling across the border or at an airport.

Right to Remain Silent

Noncitizens generally have the same right to remain silent that citizens do. If questioned by law enforcement agents, you can remain silent and refuse to answer their questions even if they detain you temporarily or arrest you. You can simply say nothing or say something like "I'd like to talk to my lawyer before I say anything to you," or "I have nothing to say to you. I will talk to my lawyer and have her/him contact you." Do not sign anything without reading and fully understanding the consequences of signing it.

One exception to this rule is if an immigration officer asks a noncitizen to provide information related to her/his immigration status; however, even in this situation, you can still state that you would like a lawyer present before you answer any questions.

The law also requires adult noncitizens who have valid immigration documents to carry these documents at all times. If an agent asks for your documents and you refuse to provide them, you can be charged with a misdemeanor.

Never show fake immigration papers or claim that you are a U.S. citizen if you are not. Instead, you should remain silent or say you would like to talk to a lawyer. Lying to a federal agent is a much more serious crime than the misdemeanor of failing to produce documents—it is better to not produce anything than to produce false documents. Also, falsely claiming to be a citizen may bar you from obtaining lawful status or citizenship in the future.

III.

THE ATTORNEY GENERAL'S GUIDELINES
FOR DOMESTIC FBI OPERATIONS

INTRODUCTION

The most recent *Attorney General's Guidelines for Domestic FBI Operations* (often called the Mukasey guidelines after U.S. Attorney General Michael Mukasey), issued in December 2008 at the end of the Bush administration and reprinted here, currently governs FBI behavior. The Obama administration has done nothing to limit the broad powers given to the FBI under those guidelines.

Prior to the issuance of the Mukasey guidelines, former attorney general John Ashcroft, a few months after 9/11, issued guidelines that provided for wholesale political spying on dissenters. The Ashcroft guidelines included the repeal of Ford administration–era guidelines that had barred the FBI from attending political meetings and houses of worship to spy on activities and individuals not suspected nor accused of any crimes. The Ashcroft guidelines instituted massive surveillance of political meetings and rallies, religious gatherings, Internet sites and bulletin

boards, and other purely expressive activities explicitly
protected by the First Amendment The Ashcroft guidelines also authorized the FBI to enter massive numbers of
names of individuals under such surveillance into government databases.

Extreme even by the Ashcroft standard, the Mukasey
guidelines do not limit the FBI but afford it such untram-
meled power that the guidelines might as well not exist.
Under the Mukasey guidelines, the FBI may investigate
anyone at all, even in the absence of any evidence whatsoever of a crime. The FBI is authorized to investigate
political demonstrations, is newly permitted to employ
a variety of intrusive investigative techniques previously
off-limits, and is actually encouraged to make aggressive
use of informants. Under these guidelines, the FBI's role
is officially expanded well beyond that of a domestic law
enforcement agency. As the Center for Democracy and
Technology concluded in its report, the Mukasey guidelines "cement the FBI's status as a domestic intelligence
agency."[1]

The Mukasey guidelines expand the FBI's mandate well
beyond its traditional role of dealing with violations of the
law. The bureau now has the authority and responsibility to investigate "threats to the national security," an ill-
defined term that has been interpreted to cover all forms
of political dissent, making the FBI into a kind of political
police. Antiwar activists can and have been construed to
represent such a threat. Because the FBI has also been given
authority under the Mukasey guidelines to gather information regarding the conduct of foreign affairs, a whole
other category of activist has also come under suspicion.
For example, a member of a group supporting an end to

the Israeli occupation of the West Bank and Gaza can now legally be investigated, as can anyone with any connection to a foreign policy issue—even a professor writing about a foreign country. As the guidelines themselves state, the FBI is entitled to obtain information related to foreign affairs even if "the information so gathered may concern lawful activities" (p. 103).

Even in its investigation of *lawful* activities, the FBI need not operate consensually under the Mukasey guidelines (although it is instructed to do so if practicable), but is permitted to use covert spying techniques developed to pursue criminal investigations. All legal authorities are available in the three areas of investigation outlined on pages 97–103.

In another example of overreaching, the Mukasey guidelines, under a section titled "General Authorities," dispense with the Privacy Act restrictions on keeping records about United States citizens and permanent residents, flatly stating that all activities authorized by the guidelines are exempt from the Privacy Act. As surveillance and the gathering of information can be carried out without any criminal predicate and on the completely innocent, these guidelines have effectively granted the FBI the authority to use and retain records on millions of law-abiding Americans (p. 109).

Likewise, in a section called "Investigations and Intelligence Gathering," the FBI is "authorized and encouraged" to identify and recruit informants even if the activities to be investigated are totally lawful. The use of informants is supposedly part of the FBI's intelligence gathering function (p. 113). But once an informant is in a group, it is not realistic to expect him or her to confine his or her activities to merely listening without raising suspicions. As a result, informants often end up participating in active ways and even suggesting tactics, some of which may be illegal—depending on what the informant's FBI handler suggests.

In a direct blow to lawful First Amendment activities, the Mukasey guidelines encourage the FBI proactively to obtain information "of possible investigative interest" on individuals and groups and to engage in surfing the Internet for almost any reason at all, including searching for individuals "who may have value as human sources," a category with no apparent limits whatsoever. Under the Mukasey guidelines, the FBI is permitted to gather information that might be helpful to foreign intelligence, meaning that anyone who voices an opinion on almost any world issue is subject to investigation, recruitment, and record keeping.

The guidelines contain various lists of authorized investigative methods (p. 120 and p. 136), many permitted without any kind of court order. Examples include: mail covers (copying the addresses on mail), opening and reading mail, physical searches of personal or real property without a warrant under certain circumstances, consensual monitoring of communications (in cases where one of the parties, such as an informant, consents), electronic surveillance, closed-circuit television surveillance, use of global positioning and other monitoring devices, National Security Letters, and more.

In one of their nastier grants of authority, the guidelines authorize undercover operations, involving the infiltration of a group by an FBI agent, without any need for a criminal predicate. The United States has a long and sordid history of such undercover operations, the consequences of which can range from changes in the political direction of an organization, to dissension, to entrapment. In contrast to long-standing precedents, undercover operations involving political and religious organizations are now authorized by the Mukasey guidelines, requiring only approval by FBI headquarters. In short, under the Mukasey guidelines, everything we do, say, and write, every demonstration we organize or in which we participate in twenty-first-century America, is subject to FBI investigation.

Note: The following guidelines are reprinted here as they appear in the document available to the public on the Web site of the U.S. Department of Justice (www.justice.gov). Though the text was typeset to adhere to the format of this book, any typographical mistakes, grammatical errors, or stylistic inconsistencies were left as is to avoid altering the document in any way.

THE ATTORNEY GENERAL'S GUIDELINES FOR DOMESTIC FBI OPERATIONS

Preamble

These Guidelines are issued under the authority of the Attorney General as provided in sections 509, 510, 533, and
534 of title 28, United States Code, and Executive Order
12333. They apply to domestic investigative activities of
the Federal Bureau of Investigation (FBI) and other activities as provided herein.

TABLE OF CONTENTS

Introduction

As the primary investigative agency of the federal government, the Federal Bureau of Investigation (FBI) has the authority and responsibility to investigate all violations of federal law that are not exclusively assigned to another federal agency. The FBI is further vested by law and by Presidential directives with the primary role in carrying out investigations within the United States of threats to the national security. This includes the lead domestic role in investigating international terrorist threats to the United States, and in conducting counterintelligence activities to meet foreign entities' espionage and intelligence efforts directed against the United States. The FBI is also vested with important functions in collecting foreign intelligence as a member agency of the U.S. Intelligence Community. The FBI accordingly plays crucial roles in the enforcement of federal law and the proper administration of justice in the United States, in the protection of the national security, and in obtaining information needed by the United States for the conduct of its foreign affairs. These roles reflect the wide range of the FBI's current responsibilities and obligations, which require the FBI to be both an agency that effectively detects, investigates, and prevents crimes, and an agency that effectively protects the national security and collects intelligence.

The general objective of these Guidelines is the full utilization of all authorities and investigative methods, consistent with the Constitution and laws of the United States, to protect the United States and its people from terrorism and other threats to the national security, to protect the United States and its people from victimization by all crimes in violation of federal law, and to further the foreign intelligence objectives of the United States. At the same time, it is axiomatic that the FBI must conduct its investigations and other activities in a lawful and reasonable manner that respects liberty and privacy and avoids unnecessary intrusions into the lives of law-abiding people. The purpose of these Guidelines, therefore, is to establish consistent policy in such matters. They will enable the FBI to perform its duties with effectiveness, certainty, and confidence, and will provide the American people with a firm assurance that the FBI is acting properly under the law.

The issuance of these Guidelines represents the culmination of the historical evolution of the FBI and the policies governing its domestic operations subsequent to the September 11, 2001, terrorist attacks on the United States. Reflecting decisions and directives of the President and the Attorney General, inquiries and enactments of Congress, and the conclusions of national commissions, it was recognized that the FBI's functions needed to be expanded and better integrated to meet contemporary realities:

[C]ontinuing coordination . . . is necessary to optimize the FBI's performance in both national security and criminal investigations. . . . [The] new reality requires first that the FBI and other agencies do a better job of gathering intelligence inside the United States, and second that we eliminate the remnants of the old "wall" between foreign intelligence and domestic law enforcement. Both tasks must be accomplished without sacrificing our domestic liberties and the rule of law, and both depend on building a very different FBI from the one we had on September 10, 2001. (Report of the Commission on the Intelligence Capabilities of the United States Regarding Weapons of Mass Destruction 466, 452 [2005].)

In line with these objectives, the FBI has reorganized and reoriented its programs and missions, and the guidelines issued by the Attorney General for FBI operations have been extensively revised over the past several years. Nevertheless, the principal directives of the Attorney General governing the FBI's conduct of criminal investigations, national security investigations, and foreign intelligence collection have persisted as separate documents involving different standards and procedures for comparable activities. These Guidelines effect a more complete integration and harmonization of standards, thereby providing the FBI and other affected Justice Department components with clearer, more consistent, and more accessible guidance for their activities, and making available to the public in a single document the basic body of rules for the FBI's domestic operations.

These Guidelines also incorporate effective oversight measures involving many Department of Justice and FBI components, which have been adopted to ensure that all FBI activities are conducted in a manner consistent with law and policy.

The broad operational areas addressed by these Guidelines are the FBI's conduct of investigative and intelligence gathering activities, including cooperation and coordination with other components and agencies in such activities, and the intelligence analysis and planning functions of the FBI.

A. FBI RESPONSIBILITIES—FEDERAL CRIMES, THREATS TO THE NATIONAL SECURITY, FOREIGN INTELLIGENCE

Part II of these Guidelines authorizes the FBI to carry out investigations to detect, obtain information about, or prevent or protect against federal crimes or threats to the national security or to collect foreign intelligence. The major subject areas of information-gathering activities under these Guidelines—federal crimes, threats to the national security, and foreign intelligence—are not distinct, but rather overlap extensively. For example, an investigation relating to international terrorism will invariably crosscut these areas because international terrorism is included under these Guidelines' definition of "threat to the national security," because international terrorism subject to investigation within the United States usually involves criminal acts that violate federal law, and because information relating to international terrorism also falls within the definition of "foreign intelligence." Likewise, counterintelligence activities relating to espionage are likely to concern matters that constitute threats to the national security, that implicate violations or potential violations of federal espionage laws, and that involve information falling under the definition of "foreign intelligence."

While some distinctions in the requirements and procedures for investigations are necessary in different subject areas, the general design of these Guidelines is to take a uniform approach wherever possible, thereby promoting certainty and consistency regarding the applicable standards and facilitating compliance with those standards. Hence, these Guidelines do not require that the FBI's information-gathering activities be differentially labeled as "criminal investigations," "national security investigations," or "foreign intelligence collections," or that the categories of FBI personnel who carry out investigations be segregated from each other based on the subject areas in which they operate. Rather, all of the FBI's legal authorities are available for deployment in all cases to which they apply to protect the public from crimes and threats to the national security and to further the United States' foreign intelligence objectives. In many cases, a single investigation will be supportable as an exercise of a number of these authorities—i.e., as an investigation of a federal crime or crimes, as an investigation of a threat to the national security, and/or as a collection of foreign intelligence.

1. Federal Crimes

The FBI has the authority to investigate all federal crimes that are not exclusively assigned to other agencies. In most ordinary criminal investigations, the immediate objectives include such matters as: determining whether a federal crime has occurred or is occurring, or if planning or preparation for such a crime is taking place; identifying, locating, and apprehending the perpetrators; and obtaining the evidence needed for prosecution. Hence, close cooperation and coordination with federal prosecutors in the United States Attorneys' Offices and the Justice Department litigating divisions are essential both to ensure that agents have the investigative tools and legal advice at their disposal for which prosecutorial assistance or approval is needed, and to ensure that investigations are conducted in a manner that will lead to successful prosecution. Provisions in many parts of these Guidelines establish procedures and requirements for such coordination.

2. Threats to the National Security

The FBI's authority to investigate threats to the national security derives from the executive order concerning U.S. intelligence activities, from delegations of functions by the Attorney General, and from various statutory sources. See, e.g., E.O. 12333; 50 U.S.C. 401 et seq.; 50 U.S.C. 1801 et seq. These Guidelines (Part VII.S) specifically define threats to the national security to mean: international terrorism; espionage and other intelligence activities, sabotage, and assassination, conducted by, for, or on behalf of foreign powers, organizations, or persons; foreign computer intrusion; and other matters determined by the Attorney General, consistent with Executive Order 12333 or any successor order.

Activities within the definition of "threat to the national security" that are subject to investigation under these Guidelines commonly involve violations (or potential violations) of federal criminal laws. Hence, investigations of such threats may constitute an exercise both of the FBI's criminal investigation authority and of the FBI's authority to investigate threats to the national security. As with criminal investigations generally, detecting and solving the crimes, and eventually arresting and prosecuting the perpetrators, are likely to be among the objectives of investigations relating to threats to the national security. But these investigations also often serve important purposes outside the ambit of normal criminal investigation and prosecution, by providing the basis for, and informing decisions concerning, other measures needed to protect the national security. These measures may include, for example: excluding or removing persons involved in terrorism or espionage from the United States; recruitment of double agents; freezing assets of organizations that engage in or support terrorism; securing targets of terrorism or espionage; providing threat information and warnings to other federal, state, local, and private agencies and entities; diplomatic or military actions; and actions by other intelligence agencies to counter international terrorism or other national security threats.

In line with this broad range of purposes, investigations of threats to the national security present special needs to coordinate with other Justice Department components, including particularly the Justice Department's National Security Division, and to share information and cooperate with other agencies with national security responsibilities, including other agencies of the U.S. Intelligence Community, the Department of Homeland Security, and relevant White House (including National Security Council and Homeland Security Council) agencies and entities. Various provisions in these Guidelines establish procedures and requirements to facilitate such coordination.

3. Foreign Intelligence

As with the investigation of threats to the national security, the FBI's authority to collect foreign intelligence derives from a mixture of administrative and statutory sources. See, e.g., E.O. 12333; 50 U.S.C. 401 et seq.; 50 U.S.C. 1801 et seq.; 28 U.S.C. 532 note (incorporating P.L. 108-458 §§ 2001–2003). These Guidelines (Part VII.E) define foreign intelligence to mean "information relating to the capabilities, intentions, or activities of foreign governments or elements thereof, foreign organizations or foreign persons, or international terrorists."

The FBI's foreign intelligence collection activities have been expanded by legislative and administrative reforms subsequent to the September 11, 2001, terrorist attacks, reflecting the FBI's role as the primary collector of foreign intelligence within the United States, and the recognized imperative that the United States' foreign intelligence collection activities become more flexible, more proactive, and more efficient in order to protect the homeland and adequately inform the United States' crucial decisions in its dealings with the rest of the world:

> The collection of information is the foundation of everything that the Intelligence Community does. While successful collection cannot ensure a good analytical product, the failure to collect information . . . turns analysis into guesswork. And as our review demonstrates, the Intelligence Community's human and technical intelligence collection agencies have collected far too little information on many of the issues we care about most. (Report of the Commission on the Intelligence Capabilities of the United States Regarding Weapons of Mass Destruction 351 [2005].)

These Guidelines accordingly provide standards and procedures for the FBI's foreign intelligence collection activities that meet current needs and realities and optimize the FBI's ability to discharge its foreign intelligence collection functions.

The authority to collect foreign intelligence extends the sphere of the FBI's information-gathering activities beyond federal crimes and threats to the national security, and permits the FBI to seek information regarding a broader range of matters relating to foreign powers, organizations, or persons that may be of interest to the conduct of the United States' foreign affairs. The FBI's role is central to the effective collection of foreign intelligence within the United States because the authorized domestic activities of other intelligence agencies are more constrained than those of the FBI under applicable statutes and Executive Order 12333. In collecting foreign intelligence, the FBI will generally be guided by nationally determined intelligence requirements, including the National Intelligence Priorities Framework and the National HUMINT Collection Directives, or any successor directives issued under the authority of the Director of National Intelligence (DNI). As provided in Part VII.F of these Guidelines, foreign intelligence requirements may also be established by the President or Intelligence Community officials designated by the President, and by the Attorney General, the Deputy Attorney General, or an official designated by the Attorney General.

The general guidance of the FBI's foreign intelligence collection activities by DNI-authorized requirements does not, however, limit the FBI's authority to conduct investi-

gations supportable on the basis of its other authorities—
to investigate federal crimes and threats to the national
security—in areas in which the information sought also
falls under the definition of foreign intelligence. The FBI
conducts investigations of federal crimes and threats to
the national security based on priorities and strategic objectives set by the Department of Justice and the FBI, inde-
pendent of DNI-established foreign intelligence collection
requirements.

Since the authority to collect foreign intelligence en-
ables the FBI to obtain information pertinent to the
United States' conduct of its foreign affairs, even if that
information is not related to criminal activity or threats
to the national security, the information so gathered may
concern lawful activities. The FBI should accordingly operate openly and consensually with U.S. persons to the extent practicable when collecting foreign intelligence that
does not concern criminal activities or threats to the national security.

B. THE FBI AS AN INTELLIGENCE AGENCY

The FBI is an intelligence agency as well as a law enforcement agency. Its basic functions accordingly extend
beyond limited investigations of discrete matters, and
include broader analytic and planning functions. The
FBI's responsibilities in this area derive from various administrative and statutory sources. See, e.g., E.O. 12333;
28 U.S.C. 532 note (incorporating P.L. 108–458 §§ 2001–
2003) and 534 note (incorporating P.L. 109–162 § 1107).
Enhancement of the FBI's intelligence analysis capabilities

and functions has consistently been recognized as a key priority in the legislative and administrative reform efforts following the September 11, 2001, terrorist attacks:

> [Counterterrorism] strategy should . . . encompass specific efforts to . . . enhance the depth and quality of domestic intelligence collection and analysis. . . . [T]he FBI should strengthen and improve its domestic [intelligence] capability as fully and expeditiously as possible by immediately instituting measures to . . . significantly improve strategic analytical capabilities. . . . (Joint Inquiry into Intelligence Community Activities Before and After the Terrorist Attacks of September 11, 2001, S. Rep. No. 351 & H.R. Rep. No. 792, 107th Cong., 2d Sess. 4–7 [2002] [errata print].)

> A "smart" government would *integrate* all sources of information to see the enemy as a whole. Integrated all-source analysis should also inform and shape strategies to collect more intelligence. . . . The importance of integrated, all-source analysis cannot be overstated. Without it, it is not possible to "connect the dots." (Final Report of the National Commission on Terrorist Attacks Upon the United States 401, 408 [2004].)

Part IV of these Guidelines accordingly authorizes the FBI to engage in intelligence analysis and planning, drawing on all lawful sources of information. The functions authorized under that Part include: (i) development of overviews and analyses concerning threats to and vulnerabilities of the United States and its interests, (ii) research and analysis to produce reports and assessments concerning matters relevant to investigative activities or other authorized FBI activities, and (iii) the operation of intelligence systems that facilitate and support investigations through the compilation and analysis of data and information on an ongoing basis.

C. OVERSIGHT

The activities authorized by these Guidelines must be conducted in a manner consistent with all applicable laws, regulations, and policies, including those protecting privacy and civil liberties. The Justice Department's National Security Division and the FBI's Inspection Division, Office of General Counsel, and Office of Integrity and Compliance, along with other components, share the responsibility to ensure that the Department meets these goals with respect to national security and foreign intelligence matters. In particular, the National Security Division's Oversight Section, in conjunction with the FBI's Office of General Counsel, is responsible for conducting regular reviews of all aspects of FBI national security and foreign intelligence activities. These reviews, conducted at FBI field offices and headquarters units, broadly examine such activities for compliance with these Guidelines and other applicable requirements.

Various features of these Guidelines facilitate the National Security Division's oversight functions. Relevant requirements and provisions include: (i) required notification by the FBI to the National Security Division concerning full investigations that involve foreign intelligence collection or investigation of United States persons in relation to threats of the national security, (ii) annual reports by the FBI to the National Security Division concerning the FBI's foreign intelligence collection program, including information on the scope and nature of foreign intelligence collection activities in each FBI field office, and (iii) access by the National Security Division to information obtained by the FBI through national security or foreign intelligence activities and general authority for the Assistant Attorney General for National Security to obtain reports from the FBI concerning these activities.

Pursuant to these Guidelines, other Attorney General guidelines, and institutional assignments of responsibility within the Justice Department, additional Department components—including the Criminal Division, the United States Attorneys' Offices, and the Office of Privacy and Civil Liberties—are involved in the common endeavor with the FBI of ensuring that the activities of all Department components are lawful, appropriate, and ethical as well as effective. Examples include the involvement of both FBI and prosecutorial personnel in the review of undercover operations involving sensitive circumstances, notice requirements for investigations involving sensitive investigative matters (as defined in Part VII.N of these Guidelines), and notice and oversight provisions for enterprise investigations, which may involve a broad examination of groups implicated in the gravest criminal and national security threats. These requirements and procedures help to ensure that the rule of law is respected in the Department's activities and that public confidence is maintained in these activities.

I. General Authorities and Principles

A. SCOPE

These Guidelines apply to investigative activities conducted by the FBI within the United States or outside the territories of all countries. They do not apply to investigative activities of the FBI in foreign countries, which are governed by the Attorney General's Guidelines for Extraterritorial FBI Operations.

B. GENERAL AUTHORITIES

1. The FBI is authorized to conduct investigations to detect, obtain information about, and prevent and protect against federal crimes and threats to the national security and to collect foreign intelligence, as provided in Part II of these Guidelines.

2. The FBI is authorized to provide investigative assistance to other federal agencies, state, local, or tribal agencies, and foreign agencies as provided in Part III of these Guidelines.

3. The FBI is authorized to conduct intelligence analysis and planning as provided in Part IV of these Guidelines.

4. The FBI is authorized to retain and share information obtained pursuant to these Guidelines as provided in Part VI of these Guidelines.

C. USE OF AUTHORITIES AND METHODS

1. Protection of the United States and Its People

The FBI shall fully utilize the authorities provided and the methods authorized by these Guidelines to protect the United States and its people from crimes in violation of federal law and threats to the national security, and to further the foreign intelligence objectives of the United States.

2. Choice of Methods

a. The conduct of investigations and other activities authorized by these Guidelines may present choices between the use of different investigative methods that are each operationally sound and effective, but that are more or less intrusive, considering such factors as the effect on the privacy and civil liberties of individuals and potential damage to reputation. The least intrusive method feasible is to be used in such situations. It is recognized, however, that the choice of methods is a matter of judgment. The FBI shall not hesitate to use any lawful method consistent with these Guidelines, even if intrusive, where the degree of intrusiveness is warranted in light of the seriousness of a criminal or national security threat or the strength of the information indicating its existence, or in light of the importance of foreign intelligence sought to the United States' interests. This point is to be particularly observed in investigations relating to terrorism.

b. United States persons shall be dealt with openly and consensually to the extent practicable when collecting foreign intelligence that does not concern criminal activities or threats to the national security.

3. **Respect for Legal Rights**

All activities under these Guidelines must have a valid purpose consistent with these Guidelines, and must be carried out in conformity with the Constitution and all applicable statutes, executive orders, Department of Justice regulations and policies, and Attorney General guidelines. These Guidelines do not authorize investigating or collecting or maintaining information on United States persons solely for the purpose of monitoring activities protected by the First Amendment or the lawful exercise of other rights secured by the Constitution or laws of the United States. These Guidelines also do not authorize any conduct prohibited by the Guidance Regarding the Use of Race by Federal Law Enforcement Agencies.

4. **Undisclosed Participation in Organizations**

Undisclosed participation in organizations in activities under these Guidelines shall be conducted in accordance with FBI policy approved by the Attorney General.

5. **Maintenance of Records Under the Privacy Act**

The Privacy Act restricts the maintenance of records relating to certain activities of individuals who are

United States persons, with exceptions for circumstances in which the collection of such information is pertinent to and within the scope of an authorized law enforcement activity or is otherwise authorized by statute 5 U.S.C. 552a(e)(7). Activities authorized by these Guidelines are authorized law enforcement activities or activities for which there is otherwise statutory authority for purposes of the Privacy Act. These Guidelines, however, do not provide an exhaustive enumeration of authorized FBI law enforcement activities or FBI activities for which there is otherwise statutory authority, and no restriction is implied with respect to such activities carried out by the FBI pursuant to other authorities. Further questions about the application of the Privacy Act to authorized activities of the FBI should be addressed to the FBI Office of the General Counsel, the FBI Privacy and Civil Liberties Unit, or the Department of Justice Office of Privacy and Civil Liberties.

D. NATURE AND APPLICATION OF THE GUIDELINES

1. Repealers

These Guidelines supersede the following guidelines, which are hereby repealed:

a. The Attorney General's Guidelines on General Crimes, Racketeering Enterprise and Terrorism Enterprise Investigations (May 30, 2002) and all predecessor guidelines thereto.

b. The Attorney General's Guidelines for FBI National Security Investigations and Foreign Intelligence Collection (October 31, 2003) and all predecessor guidelines thereto.

c. The Attorney General's Supplemental Guidelines for Collection, Retention, and Dissemination of Foreign Intelligence (November 29, 2006).

d. The Attorney General's Procedure for Reporting and Use of Information Concerning Violations of Law and Authorization for Participation in Otherwise Illegal Activity in FBI Foreign Intelligence, Counterintelligence or International Terrorism Intelligence Investigations (August 8, 1988).

e. The Attorney General's Guidelines for Reporting on Civil Disorders and Demonstrations Involving a Federal Interest (April 5, 1976).

2. Status as Internal Guidance

These Guidelines are set forth solely for the purpose of internal Department of Justice guidance. They are not intended to, do not, and may not be relied upon to create any rights, substantive or procedural, enforceable by law by any party in any matter, civil or criminal, nor do they place any limitation on otherwise lawful investigative and litigative prerogatives of the Department of Justice.

3. Departures From the Guidelines

Departures from these Guidelines must be approved by the Director of the FBI, by the Deputy Director of the FBI, or by an Executive Assistant Director designated by the Director. If a departure is necessary without such prior approval because of the immediacy or gravity of a threat to the safety of persons or property or to the national security, the Director, the Deputy Director, or a designated Executive Assistant Director shall be notified as soon thereafter as practicable. The FBI shall provide timely written notice of departures from these Guidelines to the Criminal Division and the National Security Division, and those divisions shall notify the Attorney General and the Deputy Attorney General. Notwithstanding this paragraph, all activities in all circumstances must be carried out in a manner consistent with the Constitution and laws of the United States.

4. Other Activities Not Limited

These Guidelines apply to FBI activities as provided herein and do not limit other authorized activities of the FBI, such as the FBI's responsibilities to conduct background checks and inquiries concerning applicants and employees under federal personnel security programs, the FBI's maintenance and operation of national criminal records systems and preparation of national crime statistics, and the forensic assistance and administration functions of the FBI Laboratory.

II. Investigations and Intelligence Gathering

This Part of the Guidelines authorizes the FBI to conduct investigations to detect, obtain information about, and prevent and protect against federal crimes and threats to the national security and to collect foreign intelligence.

When an authorized purpose exists, the focus of activities authorized by this Part may be whatever the circumstances warrant. The subject of such an activity may be, for example, a particular crime or threatened crime; conduct constituting a threat to the national security; an individual, group, or organization that may be involved in criminal or national security–threatening conduct; or a topical matter of foreign intelligence interest.

Investigations may also be undertaken for protective purposes in relation to individuals, groups, or other entities that may be targeted for criminal victimization or acquisition, or for terrorist attack or other depredations by the enemies of the United States. For example, the participation of the FBI in special events management, in relation to public events or other activities whose character may make them attractive targets for terrorist attack, is an authorized exercise of the authorities conveyed by these Guidelines. Likewise, FBI counterintelligence activities directed to identifying and securing facilities, personnel, or information that may be targeted for infiltration, recruitment, or acquisition by foreign intelligence services are authorized exercises of the authorities conveyed by these Guidelines.

The identification and recruitment of human sources— who may be able to provide or obtain information relating to criminal activities, information relating to terrorism, espionage, or other threats to the national security, or information relating to matters of foreign intelligence interest—is also critical to the effectiveness of the FBI's law enforcement, national security, and intelligence programs, and activities undertaken for this purpose are authorized and encouraged.

The scope of authorized activities under this Part is not limited to "investigation" in a narrow sense, such as solving particular cases or obtaining evidence for use in particular criminal prosecutions. Rather, these activities also provide critical information needed for broader analytic and intelligence purposes to facilitate the solution and prevention of crime, protect the national security, and further foreign intelligence objectives. These purposes include use of the information in intelligence analysis and planning under Part IV, and dissemination of the information to other law enforcement, Intelligence Community, and White House agencies under Part VI. Information obtained at all stages of investigative activity is accordingly to be retained and disseminated for these purposes as provided in these Guidelines, or in FBI policy consistent with these Guidelines, regardless of whether it furthers investigative objectives in a narrower or more immediate sense.

In the course of activities under these Guidelines, the FBI may incidentally obtain information relating to matters outside of its areas of primary investigative responsibility. For example, information relating to violations of state or local law or foreign law may be incidentally obtained in the course of investigating federal crimes or threats to the national security or in collecting foreign intelligence. These Guidelines do not bar the acquisition of such information in the course of authorized investigative activities, the retention of such information, or its dissemination as appropriate to the responsible authorities in other agencies or jurisdictions. Part VI of these Guidelines includes specific authorizations and requirements for sharing such information with relevant agencies and officials.

This Part authorizes different levels of information gathering activity, which afford the FBI flexibility, under appropriate standards and procedures, to adapt the methods utilized and the information sought to the nature of the matter under investigation and the character of the information supporting the need for investigation.

Assessments, authorized by Subpart A of this Part, require an authorized purpose but not any particular factual predication. For example, to carry out its central mission of preventing the commission of terrorist acts against the United States and its people, the FBI must proactively draw on available sources of information to identify terrorist threats and activities. It cannot be content to wait for leads to come in through the actions of others, but rather must be vigilant in detecting terrorist activities to the full extent permitted by law, with an eye towards early intervention and prevention of acts of terrorism before they occur. Likewise, in the exercise of its protective functions, the FBI is not constrained to wait until information is received indicating that a particular event, activity, or facility has drawn the attention of those who would threaten the national security. Rather, the FBI must take the initiative to secure and protect activities and entities whose character may make them attractive targets for terrorism or espionage. The proactive investigative authority conveyed in assessments is designed for, and may be utilized by, the FBI in the discharge of these responsibilities. For example, assessments may be conducted as part of the FBI's special events management activities.

More broadly, detecting and interrupting criminal activities at their early stages, and preventing crimes from occurring in the first place, is preferable to allowing criminal plots and activities to come to fruition. Hence, assessments may be undertaken proactively with such objectives as detecting criminal activities; obtaining information on individuals, groups, or organizations of possible investigative interest, either because they may be involved in criminal or national security–threatening activities or because they may be targeted for attack or victimization by such activities; and identifying and assessing individuals who may have value as human sources. For example, assessment activities may involve proactively surfing the Internet to find publicly accessible websites and services through which recruitment by terrorist organizations and promotion of terrorist crimes is openly taking place; through which child pornography is advertised and traded; through which efforts are made by sexual predators to lure children for purposes of sexual abuse; or through which fraudulent schemes are perpetrated against the public.

The methods authorized in assessments are generally those of relatively low intrusiveness, such as obtaining publicly available information, checking government records, and requesting information from members of the public. These Guidelines do not impose supervisory approval requirements in assessments, given the types of techniques that are authorized at this stage (e.g., perusing the Internet for publicly available information). However, FBI policy will prescribe supervisory approval requirements for certain assessments, considering such matters as the purpose of the assessment and the methods being utilized.

Beyond the proactive information-gathering functions described above, assessments may be used when allegations or other information concerning crimes or threats to the national security is received or obtained, and the matter can be checked out or resolved through the relatively non-intrusive methods authorized in assessments. The checking of investigative leads in this manner can avoid the need to proceed to more formal levels of investigative activity, if the results of an assessment indicate that further investigation is not warranted.

Subpart B of this Part authorizes a second level of investigative activity, predicated investigations. The purposes or objectives of predicated investigations are essentially the same as those of assessments, but predication as provided in these Guidelines is needed—generally, allegations, reports, facts or circumstances indicative of possible criminal or national security–threatening activity, or the potential for acquiring information responsive to foreign intelligence requirements—and supervisory approval must be obtained, to initiate predicated investigations. Corresponding to the stronger predication and approval requirements, all lawful methods may be used in predicated investigations. A classified directive provides further specification concerning circumstances supporting certain predicated investigations.

Predicated investigations that concern federal crimes or threats to the national security are subdivided into preliminary investigations and full investigations. Preliminary investigations may be initiated on the basis of any allegation or information indicative of possible criminal or national security–threatening activity, but more substantial factual predication is required for full investigations. While time limits are set for the completion of preliminary investigations, full investigations may be pursued without preset limits on their duration.

The final investigative category under this Part of the Guidelines is enterprise investigations, authorized by Subpart C, which permit a general examination of the structure, scope, and nature of certain groups and organizations. Enterprise investigations are a type of full investigations. Hence, they are subject to the purpose, approval, and predication requirements that apply to full investigations, and all lawful methods may be used in carrying them out. The distinctive characteristic of enterprise investigations is that they concern groups or organizations that may be involved in the most serious criminal or national security threats to the public—generally, patterns of racketeering activity, terrorism or other threats to the national security, or the commission of offenses characteristically involved in terrorism as described in 18 U.S.C. 2332b(g)(5)(B). A broad examination of the characteristics of groups satisfying these criteria is authorized in enterprise investigations, including any relationship of the group to a foreign power, its size and composition, its geographic dimensions and finances, its past acts and goals, and its capacity for harm.

A. ASSESSMENTS

1. Purposes

Assessments may be carried out to detect, obtain information about, or prevent or protect against federal crimes or threats to the national security or to collect foreign intelligence.

2. Approval

The conduct of assessments is subject to any supervisory approval requirements prescribed by FBI policy.

3. Authorized Activities

Activities that may be carried out for the purposes described in paragraph 1 in an assessment include:

a. seeking information, proactively or in response to investigative leads, relating to:

i. activities constituting violations of federal criminal law or threats to the national security,

ii. the involvement or role of individuals, groups, or organizations in such activities; or

iii. matters of foreign intelligence interest responsive to foreign intelligence requirements;

b. identifying and obtaining information about potential targets of or vulnerabilities to criminal activities in violation of federal law or threats to the national security;

c. seeking information to identify potential human sources, assess the suitability, credibility, or value of individuals as human sources, validate human sources, or maintain the cover or credibility of human sources, who may be able to provide or obtain information relating to criminal activities in violation of federal law, threats to the national security, or matters of foreign intelligence interest; and

d. obtaining information to inform or facilitate intelligence analysis and planning as described in Part IV of these Guidelines.

4. Authorized Methods

Only the following methods may be used in assessments:

a. Obtain publicly available information.

b. Access and examine FBI and other Department of Justice records, and obtain information from any FBI or other Department of Justice personnel.

c. Access and examine records maintained by, and request information from, other federal, state, local, or tribal, or foreign governmental entities or agencies.

d. Use online services and resources (whether non-profit or commercial).

e. Use and recruit human sources in conformity with the Attorney General's Guidelines Regarding the Use of FBI Confidential Human Sources.

f. Interview or request information from members of the public and private entities.

g. Accept information voluntarily provided by governmental or private entities.

h. Engage in observation or surveillance not requiring a court order.

i. Grand jury subpoenas for telephone or electronic mail subscriber information.

B. PREDICATED INVESTIGATIONS

1. Purposes

Predicated investigations may be carried out to detect, obtain information about, or prevent or protect against federal crimes or threats to the national security or to collect foreign intelligence.

2. Approval

The initiation of a predicated investigation requires supervisory approval at a level or levels specified by FBI policy. A predicated investigation based on paragraph 3.c. (relating to foreign intelligence) must be approved by a Special Agent in Charge or by an FBI Headquarters official as provided in such policy.

3. Circumstances Warranting Investigation

A predicated investigation may be initiated on the basis of any of the following circumstances:

a. An activity constituting a federal crime or a threat to the national security has or may have occurred, is or may be occurring, or will or may occur and the investigation may obtain information relating to the activity or the involvement or role of an individual, group, or organization in such activity.

b. An individual, group, organization, entity, information, property, or activity is or may be a target of attack, victimization, acquisition, infiltration, or recruitment in connection with criminal activity in violation of federal law or a threat to the national security and the investigation may obtain information that would help to protect against such activity or threat.

c. The investigation may obtain foreign intelligence that is responsive to a foreign intelligence requirement.

4. Preliminary and Full Investigations

A predicated investigation relating to a federal crime or threat to the national security may be conducted as a preliminary investigation or a full investigation. A predicated investigation that is based solely on the authority to collect foreign intelligence may be conducted only as a full investigation.

a. Preliminary Investigations

i. Predication Required for Preliminary Investigations

A preliminary investigation may be initiated on the basis of information or an allegation indicating the existence of a circumstance described in paragraph 3.a.–b.

ii. Duration of Preliminary Investigations

A preliminary investigation must be concluded within six months of its initiation, which may be extended by up to six months by the Special Agent in Charge. Extensions of preliminary investigations beyond a year must be approved by FBI Headquarters.

iii. Methods Allowed in Preliminary Investigations

All lawful methods may be used in a preliminary investigation except for methods within the scope of Part V.A.11.–13. of these Guidelines.

b. Full Investigations

i. Predication Required for Full Investigations

A full investigation may be initiated if there is an articulable factual basis for the investigation that reasonably indicates that a circumstance described in paragraph 3.a.–b. exists or if a circumstance described in paragraph 3.c. exists.

ii. Methods Allowed in Full Investigations
All lawful methods may be used in a full
investigation.

5. Notice Requirements

a. An FBI field office shall notify FBI Headquarters
and the United States Attorney or other appropriate Department of Justice official of the initiation
by the field office of a predicated investigation
involving a sensitive investigative matter. If the
investigation is initiated by FBI Headquarters,
FBI Headquarters shall notify the United States
Attorney or other appropriate Department of
Justice official of the initiation of such an investigation. If the investigation concerns a threat to
the national security, an official of the National
Security Division must be notified. The notice
shall identify all sensitive investigative matters
involved in the investigation.

b. The FBI shall notify the National Security Division of:

i. the initiation of any full investigation of a
United States person relating to a threat to the
national security; and

ii. the initiation of any full investigation that
is based on paragraph 3.c. (relating to foreign
intelligence).

c. The notifications under subparagraphs a. and
b. shall be made as soon as practicable, but no

later than 30 days after the initiation of an investigation.

d. The FBI shall notify the Deputy Attorney General if FBI Headquarters disapproves a field office's initiation of a predicated investigation relating to a threat to the national security on the ground that the predication for the investigation is insufficient.

C. ENTERPRISE INVESTIGATIONS

1. Definition

A full investigation of a group or organization may be initiated as an enterprise investigation if there is an articulable factual basis for the investigation that reasonably indicates that the group or organization may have engaged or may be engaged in, or may have or may be engaged in planning or preparation or provision of support for:

a. a pattern of racketeering activity as defined in 18 U.S.C. 1961(5);

b. international terrorism or other threat to the national security;

c. domestic terrorism as defined in 18 U.S.C. 2331(5) involving a violation of federal criminal law;

d. furthering political or social goals wholly or in part through activities that involve force or violence and a violation of federal criminal law; or

    e. an offense described in 18 U.S.C. 2332b(g)(5)(B) or 18 U.S.C. 43.

2. Scope

The information sought in an enterprise investigation may include a general examination of the structure, scope, and nature of the group or organization including: its relationship, if any, to a foreign power; the identity and relationship of its members, employees, or other persons who may be acting in furtherance of its objectives; its finances and resources; its geographical dimensions; and its past and future activities and goals.

3. Notice and Reporting Requirements

    a. The responsible Department of Justice component for the purpose of notification and reports in enterprise investigations is the National Security Division, except that, for the purpose of notifications and reports in an enterprise investigation relating to a pattern of racketeering activity that does not involve an offense or offenses described in 18 U.S.C. 2332b(g)(5)(B), the responsible Department of Justice component is the Organized Crime and Racketeering Section of the Criminal Division.

    b. An FBI field office shall notify FBI Headquarters of the initiation by the field office of an enterprise investigation.

c. The FBI shall notify the National Security Division or the Organized Crime and Racketeering Section of the initiation of an enterprise investigation, whether by a field office or by FBI Headquarters, and the component so notified shall notify the Attorney General and the Deputy Attorney General. The FBI shall also notify any relevant United States Attorney's Office, except that any investigation within the scope of Part VI.D.1.d of these Guidelines (relating to counterintelligence investigations) is to be treated as provided in that provision. Notifications by the FBI under this subparagraph shall be provided as soon as practicable, but no later than 30 days after the initiation of the investigation.

d. The Assistant Attorney General for National Security or the Chief of the Organized Crime and Racketeering Section, as appropriate, may at any time request the FBI to provide a report on the status of an enterprise investigation and the FBI will provide such reports as requested.

III. Assistance to Other Agencies

The FBI is authorized to provide investigative assistance to other federal, state, local, or tribal, or foreign agencies as provided in this Part.

The investigative assistance authorized by this Part is often concerned with the same objectives as those identified in Part II of these Guidelines—investigating federal

crimes and threats to the national security, and collecting foreign intelligence. In some cases, however, investigative assistance to other agencies is legally authorized
for purposes other than those identified in Part II, such
as assistance in certain contexts to state or local agencies
in the investigation of crimes under state or local law, see
28 U.S.C. 540, 540A, 540B, and assistance to foreign agencies in the investigation of foreign law violations pursuant
to international agreements. Investigative assistance for
such legally authorized purposes is permitted under this
Part, even if it is not for purposes identified as grounds for
investigation under Part II.

The authorities provided by this Part are cumulative
to Part II and do not limit the FBI's investigative activities
under Part II. For example, Subpart B.2 in this Part authorizes investigative activities by the FBI in certain circumstances to inform decisions by the President concerning
the deployment of troops to deal with civil disorders, and
Subpart B.3 authorizes investigative activities to facilitate demonstrations and related public health and safety
measures. The requirements and limitations in these provisions for conducting investigations for the specified
purposes do not limit the FBI's authority under Part II to
investigate federal crimes or threats to the national security that occur in the context of or in connection with civil
disorders or demonstrations.

A. THE INTELLIGENCE COMMUNITY

The FBI may provide investigative assistance (including operational support) to authorized intelligence activities of other Intelligence Community agencies.

B. FEDERAL AGENCIES GENERALLY

1. In General

The FBI may provide assistance to any federal agency in the investigation of federal crimes or threats to the national security or in the collection of foreign intelligence, and investigative assistance to any federal agency for any other purpose that may be legally authorized, including investigative assistance to the Secret Service in support of its protective responsibilities.

2. The President in Relation to Civil Disorders

a. At the direction of the Attorney General, the Deputy Attorney General, or the Assistant Attorney General for the Criminal Division, the FBI shall collect information relating to actual or threatened civil disorders to assist the President in determining (pursuant to the authority of the President under 10 U.S.C. 331–33) whether use of the armed forces or militia is required and how a decision to commit troops should be implemented. The information sought shall concern such matters as:

i. The size of the actual or threatened disorder, both in number of people involved or affected and in geographic area.

ii. The potential for violence.

iii. The potential for expansion of the disorder in light of community conditions and underlying causes of the disorder.

iv. The relationship of the actual or threatened disorder to the enforcement of federal law or court orders and the likelihood that state or local authorities will assist in enforcing those laws or orders.

v. The extent of state or local resources available to handle the disorder.

b. Investigations under this paragraph will be authorized only for a period of 30 days, but the authorization may be renewed for subsequent 30-day periods.

c. Notwithstanding Subpart E.2 of this Part, the methods that may be used in an investigation under this paragraph are those described in subparagraphs a.–d., subparagraph f. (other than pretext interviews or requests), or subparagraph g. of Part II.A.4 of these Guidelines. The Attorney General, the Deputy Attorney General, or the Assistant Attorney General for the Criminal Division may also authorize the use of other methods described in Part II.A.4.

3. Public Health and Safety Authorities in Relation to Demonstrations

a. At the direction of the Attorney General, the Deputy Attorney General, or the Assistant Attorney General for the Criminal Division, the FBI shall collect information relating to demonstration activities that are likely to require the federal government to take action to facilitate the activities and provide public health and safety measures with respect to those activities. The information sought in such an investigation shall be that needed to facilitate an adequate federal response to ensure public health and safety and to protect the exercise of First Amendment rights, such as:

i. The time, place, and type of activities planned.

ii. The number of persons expected to participate.

iii. The expected means and routes of travel for participants and expected time of arrival.

iv. Any plans for lodging or housing of participants in connection with the demonstration.

b. Notwithstanding Subpart E.2 of this Part, the methods that may be used in an investigation under this paragraph are those described in subparagraphs a.–d., subparagraph f. (other than pretext interviews or requests), or subparagraph g. of Part II.A.4 of these Guidelines. The Attorney

General, the Deputy Attorney General, or the Assistant Attorney General for the Criminal Division may also authorize the use of other methods
described in Part II.A.4.

C. STATE, LOCAL, OR TRIBAL AGENCIES

The FBI may provide investigative assistance to state,
local, or tribal agencies in the investigation of matters
that may involve federal crimes or threats to the national
security, or for such other purposes as may be legally
authorized.

D. FOREIGN AGENCIES

1. At the request of foreign law enforcement, intelligence, or security agencies, the FBI may conduct investigations or provide assistance to investigations by such
agencies, consistent with the interests of the United States
(including national security interests) and with due consideration of the effect on any United States person. Investigations or assistance under this paragraph must be
approved as provided by FBI policy. The FBI shall notify
the National Security Division concerning investigation
or assistance under this paragraph where: (i) FBI Headquarters approval for the activity is required pursuant to
the approval policy adopted by the FBI for purposes of
this paragraph, and (ii) the activity relates to a threat to
the national security. Notification to the National Security
Division shall be made as soon as practicable but no later
than 30 days after the approval. Provisions regarding no-

tification to or coordination with the Central Intelligence Agency by the FBI in memoranda of understanding or agreements with the Central Intelligence Agency may also apply to activities under this paragraph.

2. The FBI may not provide assistance to foreign law enforcement, intelligence, or security officers conducting investigations within the United States unless such officers have provided prior notification to the Attorney General as required by 18 U.S.C. 951.

3. The FBI may conduct background inquiries concerning consenting individuals when requested by foreign government agencies.

4. The FBI may provide other material and technical assistance to foreign governments to the extent not otherwise prohibited by law.

E. APPLICABLE STANDARDS AND PROCEDURES

1. Authorized investigative assistance by the FBI to other agencies under this Part includes joint operations and activities with such agencies.

2. All lawful methods may be used in investigative assistance activities under this Part.

3. Where the methods used in investigative assistance activities under this Part go beyond the methods authorized in assessments under Part II.A.4 of these Guidelines, the following apply:

> **a.** Supervisory approval must be obtained for the activity at a level or levels specified in FBI policy.

b. Notice must be provided concerning sensitive investigative matters in the manner described in Part II.B.5.

c. A database or records system must be maintained that permits, with respect to each such activity, the prompt retrieval of the status of the activity (open or closed), the dates of opening and closing, and the basis for the activity. This database or records system may be combined with the database or records system for predicated investigations required by Part VI.A.2.

IV. Intelligence Analysis and Planning

The FBI is authorized to engage in analysis and planning. The FBI's analytic activities enable the FBI to identify and understand trends, causes, and potential indicia of criminal activity and other threats to the United States that would not be apparent from the investigation of discrete matters alone. By means of intelligence analysis and strategic planning, the FBI can more effectively discover crimes, threats to the national security, and other matters of national intelligence interest and can provide the critical support needed for the effective discharge of its investigative responsibilities and other authorized activities. For example, analysis of threats in the context of special events management, concerning public events or activities that may be targeted for terrorist attack, is an authorized activity under this Part.

In carrying out its intelligence functions under this

Part, the FBI is authorized to draw on all lawful sources of information, including but not limited to the results of investigative activities under these Guidelines. Investigative activities under these Guidelines and other legally authorized activities through which the FBI acquires information, data, or intelligence may properly be utilized, structured, and prioritized so as to support and effectuate the FBI's intelligence mission. The remainder of this Part provides further specification concerning activities and functions authorized as part of that mission.

A. STRATEGIC INTELLIGENCE ANALYSIS

The FBI is authorized to develop overviews and analyses of threats to and vulnerabilities of the United States and its interests in areas related to the FBI's responsibilities, including domestic and international criminal threats and activities; domestic and international activities, circumstances, and developments affecting the national security; and matters relevant to the conduct of the United States' foreign affairs. The overviews and analyses prepared under this Subpart may encompass present, emergent, and potential threats and vulnerabilities, their contexts and causes, and identification and analysis of means of responding to them.

B. REPORTS AND ASSESSMENTS GENERALLY

The FBI is authorized to conduct research, analyze information, and prepare reports and assessments concerning matters relevant to authorized FBI activities, such as reports and assessments concerning: types of criminals or

criminal activities; organized crime groups; terrorism, espionage, or other threats to the national security; foreign
intelligence matters; or the scope and nature of criminal
activity in particular geographic areas or sectors of the
economy.

C. INTELLIGENCE SYSTEMS

The FBI is authorized to operate intelligence, identification, tracking, and information systems in support
of authorized investigative activities, or for such other or
additional purposes as may be legally authorized, such
as intelligence and tracking systems relating to terrorists,
gangs, or organized crime groups.

V. Authorized Methods

A. PARTICULAR METHODS

All lawful investigative methods may be used in activities
under these Guidelines as authorized by these Guidelines.
Authorized methods include, but are not limited to, those
identified in the following list. The methods identified in
the list are in some instances subject to special restrictions
or review or approval requirements as noted:

1. The methods described in Part II.A.4 of these
Guidelines.

2. Mail covers.

3. Physical searches of personal or real property where
a warrant or court order is not legally required because

there is no reasonable expectation of privacy (e.g., trash covers).

4. Consensual monitoring of communications, including consensual computer monitoring, subject to legal review by the Chief Division Counsel or the FBI Office of the General Counsel. Where a sensitive monitoring circumstance is involved, the monitoring must be approved by the Criminal Division or, if the investigation concerns a threat to the national security or foreign intelligence, by the National Security Division.

5. Use of closed-circuit television, direction finders, and other monitoring devices, subject to legal review by the Chief Division Counsel or the FBI Office of the General Counsel. (The methods described in this paragraph usually do not require court orders or warrants unless they involve physical trespass or non-consensual monitoring of communications, but legal review is necessary to ensure compliance with all applicable legal requirements.)

6. Polygraph examinations.

7. Undercover operations. In investigations relating to activities in violation of federal criminal law that do not concern threats to the national security or foreign intelligence, undercover operations must be carried out in conformity with the Attorney General's Guidelines on Federal Bureau of Investigation Undercover Operations. In investigations that are not subject to the preceding sentence because they concern threats to the national security or foreign intelligence, undercover operations involving religious or political organizations must be reviewed and approved by FBI Headquarters, with participation by the National Security Division in the review process.

8. Compulsory process as authorized by law, including grand jury subpoenas and other subpoenas, National Security Letters (15 U.S.C. 1681u, 1681v; 18 U.S.C. 2709; 12 U.S.C. 3414(a)(5)(A); 50 U.S.C. 436), and Foreign Intelligence Surveillance Act orders for the production of tangible things (50 U.S.C. 1861–63).

9. Accessing stored wire and electronic communications and transactional records in conformity with chapter 121 of title 18, United States Code (18 U.S.C. 2701–2712).

10. Use of pen registers and trap and trace devices in conformity with chapter 206 of title 18, United States Code (18 U.S.C. 3121–3127), or the Foreign Intelligence Surveillance Act (50 U.S.C. 1841–1846).

11. Electronic surveillance in conformity with chapter 119 of title 18, United States Code (18 U.S.C. 2510–2522), the Foreign Intelligence Surveillance Act, or Executive Order 12333 § 2.5.

12. Physical searches, including mail openings, in conformity with Rule 41 of the Federal Rules of Criminal Procedure, the Foreign Intelligence Surveillance Act, or Executive Order 12333 § 2.5. A classified directive provides additional limitation on certain searches.

13. Acquisition of foreign intelligence information in conformity with title VII of the Foreign Intelligence Surveillance Act.

B. SPECIAL REQUIREMENTS

Beyond the limitations noted in the list above relating to particular investigative methods, the following requirements are to be observed:

1. Contacts With Represented Persons

Contact with represented persons may implicate legal restrictions and affect the admissibility of resulting evidence. Hence, if an individual is known to be represented by counsel in a particular matter, the FBI will follow applicable law and Department procedure concerning contact with represented individuals in the absence of prior notice to counsel. The Special Agent in Charge and the United States Attorney or their designees shall consult periodically on applicable law and Department procedure. Where issues arise concerning the consistency of contacts with represented persons with applicable attorney conduct rules, the United States Attorney's Office should consult with the Professional Responsibility Advisory Office.

2. Use of Classified Investigative Technologies

Inappropriate use of classified investigative technologies may risk the compromise of such technologies. Hence, in an investigation relating to activities in violation of federal criminal law that does not concern a threat to the national security or foreign intelligence, the use of such technologies must be in conformity with the Procedures for the Use of Classified Investigative Technologies in Criminal Cases.

C. OTHERWISE ILLEGAL ACTIVITY

1. Otherwise illegal activity by an FBI agent or employee in an undercover operation relating to activity in violation of federal criminal law that does not concern a threat to the national security or foreign intelligence must be approved in conformity with the Attorney General's Guidelines on Federal Bureau of Investigation Undercover Operations. Approval of otherwise illegal activity in conformity with those guidelines is sufficient and satisfies any approval requirement that would otherwise apply under these Guidelines.

2. Otherwise illegal activity by a human source must be approved in conformity with the Attorney General's Guidelines Regarding the Use of FBI Confidential Human Sources.

3. Otherwise illegal activity by an FBI agent or employee that is not within the scope of paragraph 1 must be approved by a United States Attorney's Office or a Department of Justice Division, except that a Special Agent in Charge may authorize the following:

   a. otherwise illegal activity that would not be a felony under federal, state, local, or tribal law;
   b. consensual monitoring of communications, even if a crime under state, local, or tribal law;
   c. the controlled purchase, receipt, delivery, or sale of drugs, stolen property, or other contraband;
   d. the payment of bribes;

    e. the making of false representations in
        concealment of personal identity or the true
        ownership of a proprietary; and

    f. conducting a money laundering transaction
        or transactions involving an aggregate
        amount not exceeding $1 million.

However, in an investigation relating to a threat to the national security or foreign intelligence collection, a Special Agent in Charge may not authorize an activity that may constitute a violation of export control laws or laws that concern the proliferation of weapons of mass destruction. In such an investigation, a Special Agent in Charge may authorize an activity that may otherwise violate prohibitions of material support to terrorism only in accordance with standards established by the Director of the FBI and agreed to by the Assistant Attorney General for National Security.

    4. The following activities may not be authorized:

    a. Acts of violence.

    b. Activities whose authorization is prohibited
        by law, including unlawful investigative
        methods, such as illegal electronic
        surveillance or illegal searches.

Subparagraph a, however, does not limit the right of FBI agents or employees to engage in any lawful use of force, including the use of force in self-defense or defense of others or otherwise in the lawful discharge of their duties.

5. An agent or employee may engage in otherwise illegal activity that could be authorized under this Subpart without the authorization required by paragraph 3 if necessary to meet an immediate threat to the safety of persons or property or to the national security, or to prevent the compromise of an investigation or the loss of a significant investigative opportunity. In such a case, prior to engaging in the otherwise illegal activity, every effort should be made by the agent or employee to consult with the Special Agent in Charge, and by the Special Agent in Charge to consult with the United States Attorney's Office or appropriate Department of Justice Division where the authorization of that office or division would be required under paragraph 3, unless the circumstances preclude such consultation. Cases in which otherwise illegal activity occurs pursuant to this paragraph without the authorization required by paragraph 3 shall be reported as soon as possible to the Special Agent in Charge, and by the Special Agent in Charge to FBI Headquarters and to the United States Attorney's Office or appropriate Department of Justice Division.

6. In an investigation relating to a threat to the national security or foreign intelligence collection, the National Security Division is the approving component for otherwise illegal activity for which paragraph 3 requires approval beyond internal FBI approval. However, officials in other components may approve otherwise illegal activity in such investigations as authorized by the Assistant Attorney General for National Security.

VI. Retention and Sharing of Information

A. RETENTION OF INFORMATION

1. The FBI shall retain records relating to activities under these Guidelines in accordance with a records retention plan approved by the National Archives and Records Administration.

2. The FBI shall maintain a database or records system that permits, with respect to each predicated investigation, the prompt retrieval of the status of the investigation (open or closed), the dates of opening and closing, and the basis for the investigation.

B. INFORMATION SHARING GENERALLY

1. Permissive Sharing

Consistent with law and with any applicable agreements or understanding with other agencies concerning the dissemination of information they have provided, the FBI may disseminate information obtained or produced through activities under these Guidelines:

a. within the FBI and to other components of the Department of Justice;

b. to other federal, state, local, or tribal agencies if related to their responsibilities and, in relation to other Intelligence Community agencies, the determination whether the information is related to the recipient's responsibilities may be left to the recipient;

c. to congressional committees as authorized by the Department of Justice Office of Legislative Affairs;

d. to foreign agencies if the information is related to their responsibilities and the dissemination is consistent with the interest of the United States (including national security interests) and the FBI has considered the effect such dissemination may reasonably be expected to have on any identifiable United States person;

e. if the information is publicly available, does not identify United States persons, or is disseminated with the consent of the person whom it concerns;

f. if the dissemination is necessary to protect the safety or security of persons or property, to protect against or prevent a crime or threat to the national security, or to obtain information for the conduct of an authorized FBI investigation; or

g. if dissemination of the information is otherwise permitted by the Privacy Act (5 U.S.C. 552a).

2. Required Sharing

The FBI shall share and disseminate information as required by statutes, treaties, Executive Orders, Presidential directives, National Security Council directives, Homeland Security Council directives, and Attorney General–approved policies, memoranda of understanding, or agreements.

C. INFORMATION RELATING TO CRIMINAL MATTERS

1. Coordination With Prosecutors

In an investigation relating to possible criminal activity in violation of federal law, the agent conducting the investigation shall maintain periodic written or oral contact with the appropriate federal prosecutor, as circumstances warrant and as requested by the prosecutor. When, during such an investigation, a matter appears arguably to warrant prosecution, the agent shall present the relevant facts to the appropriate federal prosecutor. Information on investigations that have been closed shall be available on request to a United States Attorney or his or her designee or an appropriate Department of Justice official.

2. Criminal Matters Outside FBI Jurisdiction

When credible information is received by an FBI field office concerning serious criminal activity not within the FBI's investigative jurisdiction, the field office shall promptly transmit the information or refer the complainant to a law enforcement agency having jurisdiction, except where disclosure would jeopardize an ongoing investigation, endanger the safety of an individual, disclose the identity of a human source, interfere with a human source's cooperation, or reveal legally privileged information. If full disclosure is not made for the reasons indicated, then, whenever feasible, the FBI field office shall make at least limited disclosure to a law enforcement agency or agencies having jurisdiction, and full disclosure shall be made as soon as the need for restricting disclosure is no longer present. Where full disclosure is not made to the appropriate law enforcement agencies within 180 days, the FBI field office shall promptly notify FBI Headquarters in writing of the facts and circumstances concerning the criminal activity. The FBI shall make periodic reports to the Deputy Attorney General on such non-disclosures and incomplete disclosures, in a form suitable to protect the identity of human sources.

3. Reporting of Criminal Activity

a. When it appears that an FBI agent or employee has engaged in criminal activity in the course of an investigation under these Guidelines, the FBI shall notify the United States Attorney's Office or an appropriate Department of Justice Division. When it appears that a human source has engaged in criminal activity in the course of an investigation under these Guidelines, the FBI shall proceed as provided in the Attorney General's Guidelines Regarding the Use of FBI Confidential Human Sources. When information concerning possible criminal activity by any other person appears in the course of an investigation under these Guidelines, the FBI shall initiate an investigation of the criminal activity if warranted, and shall proceed as provided in paragraph 1. or 2.

b. The reporting requirements under this paragraph relating to criminal activity by FBI agents or employees or human sources do not apply to otherwise illegal activity that is authorized in conformity with these Guidelines or other Attorney General guidelines or to minor traffic offenses.

D. INFORMATION RELATING TO NATIONAL SECURITY AND FOREIGN INTELLIGENCE MATTERS

The general principle reflected in current laws and policies is that there is a responsibility to provide information as consistently and fully as possible to agencies with relevant responsibilities to protect the United States and its people from terrorism and other threats to the national security, except as limited by specific constraints on such sharing. The FBI's responsibilities in this area include carrying out the requirements of the Memorandum of Understanding Between the Intelligence Community, Federal Law Enforcement Agencies, and the Department of Homeland Security Concerning Information Sharing (March 4, 2003), or any successor memorandum of understanding or agreement. Specific requirements also exist for internal coordination and consultation with other Department of Justice components, and for provision of national security and foreign intelligence information to White House agencies, as provided in the ensuing paragraphs.

1. Department of Justice

a. The National Security Division shall have access to all information obtained by the FBI through activities relating to threats to the national security or foreign intelligence. The Director of the FBI and the Assistant Attorney General for National Security shall consult concerning these activities whenever requested by either of them, and the FBI shall provide such reports and information concerning these activities as the Assistant Attorney General for National Security may request. In addition to any reports or information the Assistant Attorney General for National Security may specially request under this subparagraph, the FBI shall provide annual reports to the National Security Division concerning its foreign intelligence collection program, including information concerning the scope and nature of foreign intelligence collection activities in each FBI field office.

b. The FBI shall keep the National Security Division apprised of all information obtained through activities under these Guidelines that is necessary to the ability of the United States to investigate or protect against threats to the national security, which shall include regular consultations between the FBI and the National Security Division to exchange advice and information relevant to addressing such threats through criminal prosecution or other means.

c. Subject to subparagraphs d and e, relevant United States Attorneys' Offices shall have access to and shall receive information from the FBI relating to threats to the national security, and may engage in consultations with the FBI relating to such threats, to the same extent as the National Security Division. The relevant United States Attorneys' Offices shall receive such access and information from the FBI field offices.

d. In a counterintelligence investigation—i.e., an investigation relating to a matter described in Part VII.S.2 of these Guidelines—the FBI's provision of information to and consultation with a United States Attorney's Office are subject to authorization by the National Security Division. In consultation with the Executive Office for United States Attorneys and the FBI, the National Security Division shall establish policies setting forth circumstances in which the FBI will consult with the National Security Division prior to informing relevant United States Attorneys' Offices about such an investigation. The policies established by the National Security Division under this subparagraph shall (among other things) provide that:

i. the National Security Division will, within 30 days, authorize the FBI to share with the United States Attorneys' Offices information relating to certain espionage investigations, as defined by the policies, unless such information is withheld because of substantial national security considerations; and

ii. the FBI may consult freely with United States
Attorneys' Offices concerning investigations
within the scope of this subparagraph during
an emergency, so long as the National Security
Division is notified of such consultation as soon
as practical after the consultation.

e. Information shared with a United States Attorney's Office pursuant to subparagraph c or d
shall be disclosed only to the United States Attorney or any Assistant United States Attorneys designated by the United States Attorney as points of
contact to receive such information. The United
States Attorneys and designated Assistant United
States Attorneys shall have appropriate security
clearances and shall receive training in the handling of classified information and information
derived from the Foreign Intelligence Surveillance Act, including training concerning the secure handling and storage of such information
and training concerning requirements and limitations relating to the use, retention, and dissemination of such information.

f. The disclosure and sharing of information by the
FBI under this paragraph is subject to any limitations required in orders issued by the Foreign Intelligence Surveillance Court, controls imposed
by the originators of sensitive material, and restrictions established by the Attorney General or
the Deputy Attorney General in particular cases.
The disclosure and sharing of information by
the FBI under this paragraph that may disclose

the identity of human sources is governed by the relevant provisions of the Attorney General's Guidelines Regarding the Use of FBI Confidential Human Sources.

2. White House

In order to carry out their responsibilities, the President, the Vice President, the Assistant to the President for National Security Affairs, the Assistant to the President for Homeland Security Affairs, the National Security Council and its staff, the Homeland Security Council and its staff, and other White House officials and offices require information from all federal agencies, including foreign intelligence, and information relating to international terrorism and other threats to the national security. The FBI accordingly may disseminate to the White House foreign intelligence and national security information obtained through activities under these Guidelines, subject to the following standards and procedures:

a. Requests to the FBI for such information from the White House shall be made through the National Security Council staff or Homeland Security Council staff including, but not limited to, the National Security Council Legal and Intelligence Directorates and Office of Combating Terrorism, or through the President's Intelligence Advisory Board or the Counsel to the President.

b. Compromising information concerning domestic officials or political organizations, or information concerning activities of United States persons intended to affect the political process in the United States, may be disseminated to the White House only with the approval of the Attorney General, based on a determination that such dissemination is needed for foreign intelligence purposes, for the purpose of protecting against international terrorism or other threats to the national security, or for the conduct of foreign affairs. However, such approval is not required for dissemination to the White House of information concerning efforts of foreign intelligence services to penetrate the White House, or concerning contacts by White House personnel with foreign intelligence service personnel.

c. Examples of types of information that are suitable for dissemination to the White House on a routine basis include, but are not limited to:

i. information concerning international terrorism;

ii. information concerning activities of foreign intelligence services in the United States;

iii. information indicative of imminent hostilities involving any foreign power;

iv. information concerning potential cyber-threats to the United States or its allies;

v. information indicative of policy positions adopted by foreign officials, governments, or powers, or their reactions to United States foreign policy initiatives;

vi. information relating to possible changes in leadership positions of foreign governments, parties, factions, or powers;

vii. information concerning foreign economic or foreign political matters that might have national security ramifications; and

viii. information set forth in regularly published national intelligence requirements.

d. Communications by the FBI to the White House that relate to a national security matter and concern a litigation issue for a specific pending case must be made known to the Office of the Attorney General, the Office of the Deputy Attorney General, or the Office of the Associate Attorney General. White House policy may specially limit or prescribe the White House personnel who may request information concerning such issues from the FBI.

e. The limitations on dissemination of information by the FBI to the White House under these Guidelines do not apply to dissemination to the White House of information acquired in the course of an FBI investigation requested by the White House into the background of a potential employee or appointee, or responses to requests from the White House under Executive Order 10450.

3. Special Statutory Requirements

a. Dissemination of information acquired under the Foreign Intelligence Surveillance Act is, to the extent provided in that Act, subject to minimization procedures and other requirements specified in that Act.

b. Information obtained through the use of National Security Letters under 15 U.S.C. 1681v may be disseminated in conformity with the general standards of this Part. Information obtained through the use of National Security Letters under other statutes may be disseminated in conformity with the general standards of this Part, subject to any applicable limitations in their governing statutory provisions: 12 U.S.C. 3414(a)(5)(B); 15 U.S.C. 1681u(f); 18 U.S.C. 2709(d); 50 U.S.C. 436(e).

VII. Definitions

A. CONSENSUAL MONITORING: monitoring of communications for which a court order or warrant is not legally required because of the consent of a party to the communication.

B. EMPLOYEE: an FBI employee or an employee of another agency working under the direction and control of the FBI.

C. FOR OR ON BEHALF OF A FOREIGN POWER: the determination that activities are for or on behalf of a foreign power shall be based on consideration of the extent to which the foreign power is involved in:

1. control or policy direction;

2. financial or material support; or

3. leadership, assignments, or discipline.

D. FOREIGN COMPUTER INTRUSION: the use or attempted use of any cyber-activity or other means, by, for, or on behalf of a foreign power to scan, probe, or gain unauthorized access into one or more U.S.-based computers.

E. FOREIGN INTELLIGENCE: information relating to the capabilities, intentions, or activities of foreign governments or elements thereof, foreign organizations or foreign persons, or international terrorists.

F. FOREIGN INTELLIGENCE REQUIREMENTS:

1. national intelligence requirements issued pursuant to authorization by the Director of National Intelligence, including the National Intelligence Priorities Framework and the National HUMINT Collection Directives, or any successor directives thereto;

2. requests to collect foreign intelligence by the President or by Intelligence Community officials designated by the President; and

3. directions to collect foreign intelligence by the Attorney General, the Deputy Attorney General, or an official designated by the Attorney General.

G. FOREIGN POWER:

1. a foreign government or any component thereof, whether or not recognized by the United States;

2. a faction of a foreign nation or nations, not substantially composed of United States persons;

3. an entity that is openly acknowledged by a foreign government or governments to be directed and controlled by such foreign government or governments;

4. a group engaged in international terrorism or activities in preparation therefor;

5. a foreign-based political organization, not substantially composed of United States persons; or

6. an entity that is directed or controlled by a foreign government or governments.

H. HUMAN SOURCE: a Confidential Human Source as defined in the Attorney General's Guidelines Regarding the Use of FBI Confidential Human Sources.

I. INTELLIGENCE ACTIVITIES: any activity conducted for intelligence purposes or to affect political or governmental processes by, for, or on behalf of a foreign power.

J. INTERNATIONAL TERRORISM:

Activities that:

1. involve violent acts or acts dangerous to human life that violate federal, state, local, or tribal criminal law or would violate such law if committed within the United States or a state, local, or tribal jurisdiction;

2. appear to be intended:

   i. to intimidate or coerce a civilian population;

   ii. to influence the policy of a government by intimidation or coercion; or

iii. to affect the conduct of a government by assassination or kidnapping; and

3. occur totally outside the United States, or transcend national boundaries in terms of the means by which they are accomplished, the persons they appear to be intended to coerce or intimidate, or the locale in which their perpetrators operate or seek asylum.

K. PROPRIETARY: a sole proprietorship, partnership, corporation, or other business entity operated on a commercial basis, which is owned, controlled, or operated wholly or in part on behalf of the FBI, and whose relationship with the FBI is concealed from third parties.

L. PUBLICLY AVAILABLE: information that has been published or broadcast for public consumption, is available on request to the public, is accessible on-line or otherwise to the public, is available to the public by subscription or purchase, could be seen or heard by any casual observer, is made available at a meeting open to the public, or is obtained by visiting any place or attending any event that is open to the public.

M. RECORDS: any records, databases, files, indices, information systems, or other retained information.

N. SENSITIVE INVESTIGATIVE MATTER: an investigative matter involving the activities of a domestic public official or political candidate (involving corruption or a threat to the national security), religious or political organization or individual prominent in such an organization, or news media, or any other matter which, in the judgment of the official authorizing an

investigation, should be brought to the attention of FBI Headquarters and other Department of Justice officials.

O. SENSITIVE MONITORING CIRCUMSTANCE:

1. investigation of a member of Congress, a federal
   judge, a member of the Executive Branch at Executive
   Level IV or above, or a person who has served in such
   capacity within the previous two years;

2. investigation of the Governor, Lieutenant Governor, or
   Attorney General of any state or territory, or a judge
   or justice of the highest court of any state or territory,
   concerning an offense involving bribery, conflict of interest, or extortion related to the performance of official duties;

3. a party to the communication is in the custody of the
   Bureau of Prisons or the United States Marshals Ser-
   vice or is being or has been afforded protection in the
   Witness Security Program; or

4. the Attorney General, the Deputy Attorney General, or
   an Assistant Attorney General has requested that the
   FBI obtain prior approval for the use of consensual
   monitoring in a specific investigation.

P. SPECIAL AGENT IN CHARGE: the Special Agent in Charge
of an FBI field office (including an Acting Special Agent in
Charge), except that the functions authorized for Special
Agents in Charge by these Guidelines may also be exercised
by the Assistant Director in Charge or by any Special Agent
in Charge designated by the Assistant Director in Charge
in an FBI field office headed by an Assistant Director, and

by FBI Headquarters officials designated by the Director of the FBI.

Q. SPECIAL EVENTS MANAGEMENT: planning and conduct of public events or activities whose character may make them attractive targets for terrorist attack.

R. STATE, LOCAL, OR TRIBAL: any state or territory of the United States or political subdivision thereof, the District of Columbia, or Indian tribe.

S. THREAT TO THE NATIONAL SECURITY:

1. international terrorism;

2. espionage and other intelligence activities, sabotage, and assassination, conducted by, for, or on behalf of foreign powers, organizations, or persons;

3. foreign computer intrusion; and

4. other matters determined by the Attorney General, consistent with Executive Order 12333 or a successor order.

T. UNITED STATES: when used in a geographic sense, means all areas under the territorial sovereignty of the United States.

U. UNITED STATES PERSON:

Any of the following, but not including any association or corporation that is a foreign power as defined in Subpart G.1.–3.:

1. an individual who is a United States citizen or an alien lawfully admitted for permanent residence;

2. an unincorporated association substantially composed of individuals who are United States persons; or

3. a corporation incorporated in the United States.

In applying paragraph 2, if a group or organization in
the United States that is affiliated with a foreign-based
international organization operates directly under the
control of the international organization and has no in-
dependent program or activities in the United States, the
membership of the entire international organization shall
be considered in determining whether it is substantially
composed of United States persons. If, however, the
U.S.-based group or organization has programs or activities separate from, or in addition to, those directed by
the international organization, only its membership in the
United States shall be considered in determining whether
it is substantially composed of United States persons. A
classified directive provides further guidance concerning
the determination of United States person status.

V. USE: when used with respect to human sources, means
obtaining information from, tasking, or otherwise operating
such sources.

Date: _____9/29/08_____   _____
                               Michael B. Mukasey
                               Attorney General

ACKNOWLEDGMENTS

This book was created in conjunction with the Center for Constitutional Rights (CCR), a legal and educational organization dedicated to advancing and protecting the rights guaranteed by the U.S. Constitution and the Universal Declaration of Human Rights.

We would like to thank the many people who made this project possible, in particular those who helped create the second section of this book, which was originally published in 1989 as a pamphlet called "If an Agent Knocks" and authored by Margaret Ratner Kunstler, Linda Backiel, Ann Marie Buitrago, and CCR's Movement Support Network. It was subsequently updated and expanded in 2009 by: Matthew Strugar, CCR staff attorney at the time and principal author; CCR staff and interns, including Lauren Melodia, Rachel Meeropol, Alison Roh Park, Qa'id Jacobs, Jeff Deutch, Arwa Fidahusein, Cathe Giffuni, Toni Holness, Carolyn Hsu, Jessica Juarez, Kenneth Kreuscher, David Mandel-Anthony, and Christina Stephenson.

We would also like to thank Diane Wachtell and Tara Grove at The New Press; Bill Quigley, Jen Nessel, and Jules Lobel at the Center for Constitutional Rights; and Leslie Cagan, Gideon Oliver, Ben Rosenfeld, and Heidi Boghosian for their help with this book.

NOTES

I. The Meaning and Importance of Dissent

1. *United States v. U.S. District Court*, 407 U.S. 297 (1972).

2. The Electronic Privacy Information Center, at Epic.org, has a good summary of this watering down of the guidelines. See http://epic.org/privacy/fbi/.

3. U.S. Department of Justice, Office of the Inspector General, "A Review of the FBI's Investigations of Certain Domestic Advocacy Groups," September 2010.

4. "Murder Charges Against Former Black Panthers Based on Convictions Extracted by Torture," *Democracy Now!* January 26, 2007.

5. Center for Constitutional Rights, "Former Black Panthers Arrested and Indicted in 1971 Homicide Charges Based on Evidence Obtained through Torture," January 23, 2007.

6. Marilyn Bechtel, "Nobel Winners: 'Drop Charges Against San Francisco 8,'" *People's Weekly World*, December 8, 2007.

7. John Mangels, "Campus Shootings Helped to Change Police Tactics for Demonstrations," *Cleveland Plain Dealer,* May 2, 2010.

8. Bill Quigley, "Our Right to Dissent Is Under Siege: Why the Protests in Pittsburgh Are a Victory for Free Speech," AlterNet, September 23, 2009, http://www.alternet.org/rights/142828/our_right_to_dissent_is_under_siege:_why_the_protests_in_pittsburgh_are_a_victory_for_free_speech/.

II. If an Agent Knocks

1. At the time of publishing, the following states have some version of a stop-and-identify statute: Alabama, Arizona, Arkansas, Colorado, Delaware, Florida, Georgia, Illinois, Indiana, Kansas, Louisiana, Missouri,

Montana, Nebraska, Nevada, New Hampshire, New Mexico, New York, North Dakota, Ohio, Rhode Island, Utah, Vermont, and Wisconsin.

III. The Attorney General's Guidelines for Domestic FBI Operations

1. See http://www.edt.org/policy/investigative-guidelines-cement -fbi-role-domestic-intelligence-agency-raising-new-privacy-cha.